On Marketing

The definitive guide
for
Small Business Owners

Michael W. DeLon

—Disclaimer—

While the author has used his best efforts in preparing this book, he makes no representation or warranties with respect to accuracy or completeness of the contents of this book. The advice and strategies contained herein may not be suitable for your situation. You should consult a professional where appropriate. The author shall not be liable for any loss of profit or any other special, incidental, consequential or other damages. The purchaser or reader of this publication assumes responsibility for the use of these materials and information. Adherence to all applicable laws and regulations, both advertising and all other aspects of doing business in the United States or any other jurisdiction, is the sole responsibility of the purchaser of reader.

ISBN-13: 978-1511412056
ISBN-10: 1511412054

What Others Are Saying

"What Michael brings to the table is the ability to bring you from thinking about yourself to thinking more about your customer. Wow! What a concept. You will have to lay aside ALL of your former preconceptions about marketing, but in the end Michael has the right view to grow your business."

Mike Davidson
Parkway Automotive
Little Rock, AR

"Michael has crafted a simple solution for a complex problem: Growing and maintaining a business using a rifle rather than a shotgun. He shares his knowledge about marketing in a way that even the accountants will be excited about marketing. Thanks for sharing Michael!"

Joseph "Big Joe" Clark
The Financial Enhancement Group
Anderson, IN

"No one needs a drill bit, they need a hole! Michael breaks it down so everyone can relate, understand, learn and implement something new without breaking the bank or starting all over!"

Ryan Minick
The 2 Mortgage Guys
Kokomo, IN

"What Michael is offering is a chance to build your business. As a friend for over 20 years, I've observed Michael live out his convictions–both personally and professionally. He is a man of high integrity, and is completely prepared in all his endeavors. I highly recommend Michael as a professional coach in marketing."

Tom Cates
The Wellington Group
Indianapolis, IN

"Michael DeLon delivers! This book is filled with practical and proven strategies you can use to grow your business no matter where you start or where you wish to go.

Throughout the book, Michael talks about how to CORRECTLY market your business! In fact, I've used many of these same tactics and strategies to grow and sustain my contracting business. This book is a great testament of how to do marketing right! You should READ it! Then APPLY it!

Thank you Michael for this book."

Dean Perkins
Perkins Painting
Newton, CT

"Michael is an Out-of-the-Box thinker who will cause you to view marketing and business from a different perspective.

On Marketing is packed full of practical, where the rubber meets the road, material. No Pie-in-the-Sky thinking here, just good, practical direction to help your marketing efforts become more fruitful than you even hoped for as you began your journey.

Read this book! Read it from cover to cover and keep it on your desk as a daily reference. It will help you move from a marketing wanna-be to a marketing success story."

Roger Best
BizTek Connection
Little Rock, AR

Acknowledgements

Thank You!... for reading On Marketing.

I appreciate you investing your time to learn how to become a better marketer, to serve your customers more fully and to grow your business. I wrote this NOT to be a dust collector, but as a resource to you – the business owner, salesperson, entrepreneur or practitioner. I've invested many hours putting this together, but it wouldn't mean a thing if YOU were not reading it. So Thank You!

BUT IT DOESN'T STOP THERE...

I also want to say "Thank You!" to those who have made this book possible. You and I both know that a project like this doesn't happen by itself. It really does take an entire village.

First, to my Lord and Savior Jesus Christ. He is the One who gave me the abilities to help you grow your business and to put these concepts on paper. **Then** to my wife since 1990, Jill. You are "my love" and a constant source of encouragement, motivation and hope. **Next** there's Caleb, my eldest son. Thanks for editing this. You are an amazing young man with a bright future. **And of course** Jeremy, my youngest son. You are becoming quite the salesperson, editor and marketer. I thoroughly enjoy our discussions.

Finally, Mike Davidson – Thanks for giving me a chance when I was just getting started and for being open to my seemingly strange marketing ideas. Your continual support and encouragement means more to me than you will ever know.

Table of Contents

SECTION 1

A New Chapter in Life

I was at a point in my career when I knew it was about time for a change. I walked to the library in my home and I pulled out one of my favorite marketing books. As I turned the pages I knew that this was my future. I was finally going to live my dream.

I love the world of marketing and advertising. It's a fascinating world that allows you to really apply your creative juices, to stand apart from your competition, and to learn how to communicate your message clearly and compellingly to a prospect so they will start doing business with you. I've read a lot of definitions for marketing and most of them are more confusing than clarifying. So, in order to provide some clarity for my clients, I came up with my own definition:

> Marketing is Everything You Do
> to GAIN and RETAIN a Customer.

When I walked into my library that day, I didn't pick up just any book. I looked for a book from one of my favorite marketing experts, Jay Abraham. He has been helping small business owners with their marketing and advertising for many, many years and has a great track record. But I would not know all of that, or who Jay was at all, unless he had published his book. And it's *because* he published a book that many now consider him an "expert", including me.

So whom do you turn to for "expert advice"? When you have a question or a problem that you need to solve, or perhaps are facing a quandary for which you need some direction, where do you go? Whom do you turn to? Who might you find on your library shelves that you consider an "expert" in your life?

We all have experts we turn to from time to time. They may be in your personal life concerning finances, insurance, and legal advice; or they may be in your professional life concerning process, time management, and sales. There's an expert in most every field; people like Bob Vila in home repair to Jerry Baker with gardening to Dave Ramsey for debt-free living to the late Zig Ziglar for sales. They are all *perceived* as experts because they published a book—and now you can too.

Our process allows you publish a physical book in less than 24 hours of your time without the hassle of laboring in front of a computer screen typing and editing. We've perfected a method that removes every barrier to publishing your book and allows you to retain all of the control of your message, all of the intellectual property rights, and all of the profits.

We are a "royalty-free" publisher focused on helping you grow your business.

We help you take your ideas and turn them into a book without writing. Our proprietary *Speak-To-Write* system is simple, easy and very fast. You'll be amazed at how quickly you can get your ideas out of your head and onto the written page.

But writing a book is about a whole lot more than just having a book. We also provide you with proven marketing strategies to promote your book, and yourself as an expert who can be trusted. This positions you uniquely in the market and will help you to **Attract** new customers, **Engage** more profitably with your current customers, **Retain** existing customers and **Stimulate** referrals automatically.

> Having your own book will position you uniquely and help you build trust quickly to grow your business.

Chapter 2

Being Perceived as "The Expert"

When you hand a copy of your book to a prospect, you'll be able to have a one-on-one conversation with them *without* being present. Then, when you *do* have your first meeting, *they will be pre-disposed to do business with you because* they've been able to bond with you through the pages of your book. You'll have already "set the stage" and will have defined the "rules of engagement" so that they begin to "speak your vocabulary" (which we also help you create).

Plus, you'll have already answered many of their questions and overcome their purchasing resistance. Instead of being what Dan Kennedy calls "an unwelcome pest", you have now positioned yourself as a "welcome guest."

They will perceive you as the expert (because you wrote the book) and they'll desire to do business with *you* versus your competitors who only gave them a brochure. You'll very quickly gain market share and greater credibility. This all happens when you become an author and publish your book.

As a marketing strategist, my clients look to me to help position them in a "category of one" so they will be perceived differently from everyone else. Now, there are a variety of ways to do this (many of which you'll learn as you read this book), but the way I like best is to position my client as an expert through authorship.

I prefer this strategy because experts have more authority (what they say holds weight), they are more credible (the media loves to interview and get sound bites from experts who are credible sources), and they are called upon for their expertise in their chosen field. **Without question, the fastest, easiest, and most profitable way to become an expert is to publish your own book.**

As you look around our society, experts have books. They're the people we look to when we need counsel or advice. They're whom we go to when we have a problem or need a solution (like I did when I knew a change was coming). That's why it's so important for local business owners to position themselves as experts.

> Being recognized as the *most credible source* of information in your industry is, by far, the best way to dominate your market and grow your business.

And when you put the word "Author" after your name, you most definitely command attention.

Most business owners fight for the attention of the public through traditional media and online venues. These are all important and valuable, but they are also very crowded and it's difficult to differentiate yourself.

> When you hand someone a copy of your book, you immediately step outside the traditional battle ground and establish yourself as someone who has something to say… and who should be listened to.

This makes all the difference in the world.

Chapter 3

Winning the Battle

In their legendary book, *Positioning*, marketing experts and authors Al Ries and Jack Trout tell us that:

> **"Marketing is a battle for position in the mind of the customer."**

Handing your prospect a copy of your book (especially a personally signed copy) immediately puts you in a more favorable position.

Until now, publishing a book was out of reach for most small business owners. Large publishers want nothing to do with you, and even if they did show some interest, you'd still have to labor for hours and days and months writing your book and getting it into a form that you could submit to them, only to be rejected time after time.

Or you could go the self-publishing route that has become more popular recently. The problem with this route is that you still have to spend hours and days and weeks laboring in front of your computer typing away night after night, day after day. Who has time for that? Then, once you have your thoughts out of your head, now you have to go through dozens of pages to edit, proofread, add pictures, think about a title, create a cover, and secure an ISBN number along with a dozen other little details. And you still need to find someone to publish your book. And if you have issues or questions during this process, you have the privilege of asking friends, searching online or reading a forum looking for an answer. And if you do choose to use an online publisher, instead of talking with someone in person, most times you are required to submit a "help desk ticket" hoping someone will get back with you in 24-48 hours. Ever been there???

After I went through this entire process to publish my own book (the one you are holding in your hands right now) I finally understood why more business owners don't publish their own book. The process can be a nightmare! Who has time for all of this?

One day as I was spending some time in prayer seeking a way to grow my business and help local business owners grow their companies, the Lord gave me the idea to help business owners bridge the gap between having an idea for a book and actually getting one published. That idea has now become *Paperback Expert*.

Chapter 4

Simplifying the Process

I took that idea and transformed it into a business with its own *proprietary process that removes all of the hurdles to publishing your book, yet allows you to retain full control and all of the profits.*

The website was designed (www.PaperbackExpert.com), we created the process, wrote the documents, ordered business cards and implemented our marketing plan. What a blur of activity!

As the dust settled, what appeared was a process where we work with you to outline your book and design it from cover to cover. We then employ our proprietary *Speak to Write* system to capture your book in audio form. From there we transcribe, proofread and edit your book until it's in final form.

You are involved throughout the process, but we are doing most of the heavy lifting. In less than 24 hours of your time (and 3-4 months of our time) you'll be holding your own book in your hands, seeing your book on Amazon and reading your book on your Kindle.

This is where we move into the Promote stage of our process and provide you with proven marketing strategies to attract new customers, retain existing customers and stimulate referrals like never before.

Being an author is great, but if you don't use your book to grow your business it's all for naught. We teach you many strategies that you can use to grow your business as you position yourself as a trusted authority and expert in your market.

We actually tie a portion of our business growth to your success. Our desire is to be more than simply the publisher of you book. We want to be a partner who helps facilitate growth in your company.

Becoming an author is one of the most rewarding (and profitable) marketing strategies available to you.

You've probably thought about writing a book at some point in your life... *Now* You Can!

Learn how easy (and affordable) it is for you to build trust by putting your message in your own book. Connect with us and let's discuss how you can become a *Paperback Expert*.

Call to Request a FREE

30-Minute Author Consultation

(501) 539-0038

Chapter 5

Getting Started

Once I had everything in place, it was time to embark on my own marketing strategy. I decided to begin with the basics–face to face.

I knew that I needed to meet some business owners and others who know business owners. As I was considering my options (there are many places where business people gather), I decided to visit a few BNI groups. After visiting 5 groups in 3 weeks, I realized that this was a great organization and most definitely the right place for me.

Within three weeks, I had met with a number of people, and four of them chose to begin the process of becoming a *Paperback Expert*.

Since that time, our company has continued to see rapid growth as we are helping business owners build trust as they tell their story in a new and exciting way. We are managing the growth and expanding our team to ensure that we continually provide superior customer service and an excellent product. We take what we do very seriously because as a *Paperback Expert*, your name is on the line—and so is ours.

In addition to *Paperback Expert*, I also help our authors learn and apply proven marketing strategies to grow their business. By participating in The Authors Roundtable—an author-only marketing mastermind—our clients connect with other authors, hear what's working, share what they are experiencing and implement new ideas monthly.

On Marketing gives you proven marketing strategies that you can apply to your business, gain market share and grow your profits.

In this Newly Revised and Expanded Edition, I've included another book I've written to help you more fully understand how becoming a *Paperback Expert* can help you increase your business. I trust that by reading *10 Ways to Grow Your Business With Your Own Book* you'll benefit greatly as you consider how you can apply this marketing strategy to your business.

Should you decide that you'd like to build trust through authorship and become "the expert" in the eyes of your prospects, I invite you to contact us and learn more about our process and how becoming a *Paperback Expert* can help you grow your business. We're happy to talk with you and answer all of your questions.

I look forward to serving you…and seeing *your* name on the cover of *your* own book!

Michael

SECTION 2

10 Ways to Grow Your Business With Your Own Book

How to Quickly Establish Trust, Attract More Customers and Position Yourself as The Expert With Your Own Book.

Michael W. DeLon
Copyright © 2015 Michael W. DeLon

Dear future author,

Congratulations on taking this step to more fully understand how having your own book can help you grow your business. Having your name on the cover of your own book immediately establishes you as an Authority, increases your Credibility and positions you as an Expert. And most everyone wants to do business with an expert!

There are dozens of ways you can use a book to grow your business. In the following pages I have distilled for you 10 Ways to Grow Your Business With Your Own Book.

Over the next few minutes, you'll learn what other successful business owners, CEOs and business gurus know: how to grow your business by establishing yourself as an expert. It all begins when you put your name on your own book.

Position Yourself to Profit,

Michael W. DeLon
President | Paperback Expert

❶ Magnetize Clients with Cheese

As a business owner, you'll always be attracting new customers. But instead of chasing after customers who always seem to be eluding your grasp (like a cat chasing a mouse), wouldn't you prefer to work with customers who are drawn to you because they want what you have to offer (like a mouse being drawn to cheese)?

To grow your business, you want to become magnetic to your ideal type of customer. But how?

To do this, you need to develop a "lead generation magnet" that will attract exactly the right type of customer. As you attract them, many will enter your funnel and some will become clients.

But you need to have the right magnet, or bait. When you do, you'll attract who you want and repel the rest. And *that* is one of the secrets to effective marketing. Targeting the right market.

By using your book to attract customers, you won't spend nearly so much time, energy or money chasing after them. Your costs will diminish and your results will increase.

Using your book as a lead generation magnet is one of the first strategies we teach our clients. By offering prospects a physical copy of your book, you are inviting them to have a conversation with you without you being present.

They'll feel no pressure when they are holding your book in their hands. As they turn the pages they is no sales resistance. In fact, many times they are nodding in agreement and find themselves bonding with you emotionally.

Through reading your book, they come to know, like and trust you. You become more than just "one of the many" who do what you do. You become their ally. They feel comforatable with you. They're taking small steps *toward* you. All this is happening when you are not present physically.

Every time they see your book on their office desk or end table, they think of you. They remember their situation and know you have a solution. When they're ready to take the next step, you are the first person they contact.

Let me give you an example.

Carl Sewell is the CEO of Sewell Automotive in Dallas Texas. In 1990 Carl published a book titled, "Customers for Life."

Every prospect that walked into a Sewell Cadillac dealership received a complimentary copy of Mr. Sewell's book, even if they were "just looking." As you can imagine, many of those prospects read, or at least glanced through, that book. As they did, they learned of Sewell's 10 Commandments of Customer Service. After reading his book they realized they wouldn't receive that type of service anywhere else, and they chose to purchase their vehicles from Sewell.

Interestingly enough, in 1991 when Sewell published his book, he had three dealerships in the Dallas area. Today, Sewell has over 20 dealerships scattered around Dallas, Fort Worth, San Antonio and the surrounding areas. Do you think his book had anything to do with his success and growth? (I certainly do.)

How could you leverage your book to acquire new clients?

- First, hold a Author Signing Party for your clients. Give a signed copy of your book to them and the friends they bring.
- Second, mail or personally deliver a copy of your book to every client who does not attend your appreciation party.
- Third, give two extra copies of your book every satisfied client to give to their friends. They'll enjoy telling others they work with person who "wrote the book" on your topic.
- Fourth, give a copy of your book to key influencers in your community, along with organizations and associations you are affiliate with.
- Fifth, offer your book for free on your website. You'll need to capture their name and mailing address in this

process, which will allow you to send other materials to them in the future.

- Finally, if you have a retail business, give a copy of your book to every serious customer who enters your doors. If Carl Sewell can do it, why can't you?

There are limitless ways to use your book to grow your business. If you act like a the typical cat, you're going to chase away a lot of prospects. However, if you'll use some cheese, you'll easily lure your prospects into your funnel so you can educate and motivate them to make the intelligent decision of working with you.

When you're the author of your own book, you'll be able to attract clients more easily.

❷ End the Marketing Water Torture

3:00 a.m. Tuesday night.
I'm laying in bed, wide awake, ready to come unglued.
"This has got to stop!"
Drip, drip, drip.

A faulty washer on our kitchen sink was allowing just enough water to seep through to create a cacophany of sound, one droplet at a time.

I felt like a helpless captive to this never-ending water torture. Ever been there?

A similar feeling can overtake you when you lie awake at night thinking about how to generate more business. Should you use radio? Run a TV commercial? How about direct mail or magazine ads? Pay per click works for some. Or perhaps a simple email.

Drip, drip, drip.

One of the best ways to escape this torture chamber is to take consistent action and give your prospects what they're looking for. You know they are searching for information. You have the answers. Provide them with the information they need and gain an opportunity to educate them and become a resource to them.

We recommend you use your book to offer free information to people searching for answers. This gives them valuable information and allows you to build your mailing list—both email and physical.

Offer to send your book free of charge to anyone who is interested. You may want to pre-qualify them a bit, or ask them to pay a small shipping and handling fee to help defray the cost. If they're a good prospect and are really interested in what you provide, they'll be willing to part with a few dollars to get your book. It's really a no-brainer, especially since a book has real perceived value.

Some offer a free ebook. That's ok, but it's not as good as capturing their full contact information, which you'll need if you are to mail them a physical copy of your book.

This process will help you to identify them as a key prospect, and now you have their name and contact information so you can follow up with more specific and targeted direct mail. Perhaps you could send them a company brochure, or invite them to an upcoming event or make them some other special offer that you have.

Using your book to build your mailing list is a great way to increase your sales and grow your business. This will also result in lowering your cost per lead and cost per sale.

The other benefit of using your book to generate quality leads is that it will put an end to the water torture so many endure due to the slow drip of marketing without a compelling offer.

Let the others be driven crazy.

You can build your list by offering your book for free to those searching for answers. Don't hold back. Become their hero. Earn their trust. Grow your business.

It begins when you fix the leak in your marketing by putting your name on your own book.

❸ Be Different

The best companies in the world are different.

What makes the Disney parks stand head and shoulders above every other theme park on earth? For Disney it is cleanliness.

People go to Disney and are amazed at how clean the park is. They have a wonderful time and build great memories. Then, when they get back home, they tell their friend about the experiences they had, and they always talk about Disney's cleanliness.

How clean the park is? Yes!

That is a difference maker for Disney. And it's the differentiating factor that has made Disney millions and millions of dollars.

In today's crowded environment it is more difficult than ever to stand out in a crowd and differentiate yourself from everyone else.

Did you know that there are over 7 billion people on Earth? But only about 3 million of those are are published authors. Becoming an author puts you in the top 0.05% of people in the world!

As an author you gain instant credibility in the eyes of your customers, the media and even your competitors.

- What are you doing to differentiate yourself so that your prospects choose you over every other option they have available?
- What is it that makes you unique?
- How are you positioning yourself and your company to exceed the expectations of your customer?

Being an author tells your prospects that you have taken the time and have made the investment to go the extra mile—and that'll pay for itself time and time again.

Going that extra mile is, many times, just enough to tip the scales in your favor and send a flood of new customers your way.

Being an author is the easiest way to differentiate yourself in a very crowded marketplace.

Are you going to take that step and position yourself above the crowd like Disney has, or will you wait for one of your competitors to get there first and play "catch-up" for the rest of your life?

It's not difficult to be different. It simply takes some thought, a plan and consistent action. When you choose to create your own book you place yourself in a different category in the mind of your prospects and clients. People want to work with experts. And in our society, experts have books.

Invest the time and resources to do what you've thought about doing for so long. Become an author. Put your name on the cover of your book. When you do, you'll soon experience what Disney experiences every month. More traffic. More customers. More profit.

It starts when you choose to be different.

❹ Say "Thanks" and Retain Your Customers

Every business owner knows that it costs 7 to 10 times more money to gain a new customer then it does to retain a customer.

What are you doing to retain customers?

Have you heard of the Pareto principle? This is where 80% of your results come from 20% of your efforts. Using that as a standard, we oftentimes find that 80% of tax dollars are paid by 20% of the taxing population. Or, that 80% of your profits come from 20% of your clients.

That being the case, what are you currently doing to say "Thank You!" to the 20% of your best customers?

Try giving them a copy of your book! Books make great client appreciation gifts and are a terrific customer retention tool. A book is a wonderful tool to create customer "stickiness" and retention.

Not only does the book communicate thoughtfulness on your end, it also provides a perfectly scripted message to get in front of your clients, and their friends. Your book is a great customer thank you strategy and a superb way to help you retain and build customers for life.

Always remember it costs much less to keep a customer than it does to gain a new one. Create your book and give a copy to every customer you have. And be sure to sign it with a personal note saying, "Thank you!"

❺ Generate More Referrals

What percentage of your business comes from referrals? Truth be told, it is probably far less than you would like to believe.

Studies have shown that approximately 20% of your customers will refer you to others. Another 20% won't give referrals at all. That leaves 60% who probably would refer you, if you'd only ask and make it easy for them to do so.

The most profitable companies report that over 70% of new customers come from referrals. And with the cost of advertising and marketing continuing to go up while not producing adequate results, referrals are your best and most cost effective marketing tool.

Smart business owners give a copy of their book to every customer and ask them to hand it out to their friends, neighbors, relatives and business associates. This immediately increases your sphere of influence without costing you much money at all.

Publishing a book instantly creates a "conversation starter" with customers and their friends. You've just made it super easy for your best customers to refer you to their friends—who are people just like them. The other big deal here is that when they give out your book, you control the message being sent.

No one can tell your story better than you. Without a book, you never know what may be said about you. With your book in their hands, you are 100% certain that your message will be delivered exactly as you desire every time.

Give copies of your book to your best customers and ask them to simply pass it along to others. Doing this ensures that you control 100% of the message and you'll expand your influence more quickly for much less cost.

❻ Get Free Media Exposure

What's the fastest way to get local news media to look at your business and feature you in newspaper, on TV and radio?

Almost every business owner would love to be featured in a magazine or on TV, but for most that remains just a dream. The media doesn't care about you; they only care about delivering good content to their audience. They want a great story; and your book can be a great story.

Being an author makes you an expert. It also makes you a credible source. Reporters are constantly looking to interview experts for their stories. Publishing a book positions you in the eyes of the media favorably, and puts you on the top of their list as a place to go for comment and opinion for future articles and interviews.

Whether you are talking about TV, radio, newspaper or online coverage, being an expert will get you noticed, and then it will get you more business. Would you like to be running a monthly article in your largest trade journal? Your book could be your ticket in.

If you desire to grow your business, becoming a darling of the media is a great way. To do that, you need a story. That story is your book. The adage is truer now than ever before:

Publish, or perish.

❼ Multiply Yourself

As a business owner, you are busy. Your to-do list never goes away. You have too much to do and too little time. How in the world are you supposed to get your message out to so many people?

A book allows you to be in multiple places at once. Like mass media, publishing a book gives you greater coverage in less time (and for a much smaller investment than traditional media channels). You should be actively looking for, and taking advantage of, the most profitable distribution channels available to you. Your book is a great channel to deliver your message exactly as you desire.

As an author, you can leverage your time by talking with multiple people *at the same time.* You can give your book to people at meetings, social clubs, the country club or at an event. Even in an elevator when you have even less time, instead of handing them your business card, give them a copy of your book. Then when you walk away, they are left with your complete message in their hand.

Growing your business is not about addition, but multiplication.

If you want to take your business to the next level, you need to work smart, not just hard. Multiply yourself and your message by through the pages of your own book. Every time you give one away you will multiply your returns.

It's simple math. You just need to multiply yourself.

❽ Return to Me

One of my favorite movies is "Return to Me." Yes, it's a romantic comedy, but it's a powerful and funny movie that our family enjoys.

In marketing, I want my investments to return to me as well. So do you. I've spent far too much money on advertising that didn't have a positive ROI. So have you.

Having your own book can be the most cost-effective marketing that you ever do. A book will become the most powerful marketing tools in your arsenal, and oftentimes, the most cost-effective.

Do you know your cost per lead? What about your cost per client? Most small business owners don't know these numbers. Unless you are really tracking and managing your return on investment your marketing efforts are most likely woefully underperforming… and you'll never know why.

Your book works for you as an image advertisement, a brand builder, a high-powered business card, a direct response advertisement and a terrific credibility builder all in one. For about 5 dollars per unit, your book can do a lot of heavy lifting for your business.

A book is a phenomenal tool and provides the leverage to take you to the next level in your business. When you're an author, you'll see your investment return to you multiple times. Unlike other media that are here today and gone tomorrow, your book has shelf life.

In a few months, and definitely over time, your book will become your most effective marketing tool.

As marketing expert Bill Glazer once said,

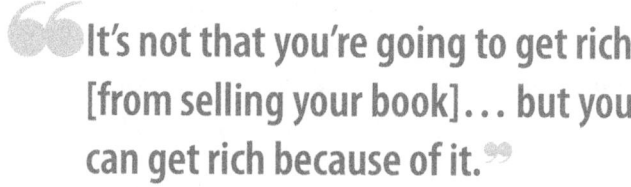

It's not that you're going to get rich [from selling your book]… but you can get rich because of it.

When you make the decision to publish your own book, you can rest assured that every marketing dollar you spend on it will "return to you."

❾ No Rest for...Your Book

The problem with business is that it gives you no rest. There are always things to do and people to see. Your task list grows faster than you can knock it out and your are constatly being interrupted. There seemingly is "no rest for the weary."

Want to know a secret?

It doesn't have to be that way.

Smart business owners have learned how to multiply their presence and increase sales without adding more complexity or salespeople. It occurs when you become an author.

There are only a couple of ways to grow your business.

1. Acquire new customers.

2. Gain repeat business.

Both of these add more sales and profits to the bottom line.

With that said, would you be interested in a proven way to increase your sales without adding salespeople?

Publish your own book.

Your book allows you to be in multiple places at the same time. It allows you to have a personal conversation with multiple people without you having to be there. When a customer or prospect is reading your book, they are focused solely on you and your message, making it a lot easier to communicate your message, establish trust and gain their commitment.

Savvy marketers will also include direct response techniques, bounce back pieces, and special offers within their book to keep the phone ringing and their lead pipeline full. A book is a cost effective direct response marketing tool that when used properly will turn on the flow of new leads, help you increase sales and grow your revenue without adding overhead or salespeople. Best of all, books don't take 2-hour lunches nor do they talk back or call in sick.

Publishing a book is your fast track to business growth. You'll quickly realize increased sales without adding staff or hiring more salespeople. Your book will be working when you're not. Prospects will read your book at night and on weekends. When you are with your family, your book is working for you.

If you're tired of the hectic pace of the rat race, then do something about it. Become an author and allow your book to work tirelessly bringing you new clients who are searching for the solutions you provide. You book will do this happily, while requiring absolutely no rest.

⑩ Basic Business

One of the first items every new employee receives is a set of business cards. Next to their name plate, this becomes their primary identifier.

What does your business card look like and how do you use it? Most likely, it looks similar to every other business card. That's unfortunate.

I think your business card should be different. I think your business card should be your book.

When you meet a prospect, what's the first thing you do when you sit down in person? You hand them your business card, right? I want you to start thinking about handing them a copy of your book instead. Using your book as your business card in your initial meeting changes the entire dynamic of your meeting and relationship.

You could say something like this,

"Mr. Prospect, thank you so much for spending a few minutes with me today. I really appreciate you making time to meet with me. As a small token of my appreciation, I would like for you to have a copy of my latest book. I think you will really enjoy it."

Now when you say that, two BIG things will normally happen:

- First, your prospect will sit up in his chair and take great interest in everything else you have to say. As an Author, your status in their eyes immediately goes up. You must be an expert!
- Second, your prospect is now in a completely different state of mind. Think about it; how many people are they meeting with who have written their own book? Probably none. You are now positioned uniquely. You are perceived as an expert. And experts are to be listened to because they have something to say.

Rather than handing prospects a standard looking business card from across the table, start handing them a signed copy of your book. You'll begin to see big changes in how you are perceived, and more importantly, in your sales.

Your book will be the most profitable business card you've ever created. It becomes your standard "calling card" and positioning piece. Your book should be the fundamental component of your marketing and how you go engage in basic business.

What Next?

I hope you have enjoyed reading 10 Ways To Grow Your Business With Your Own Book. You've just begun to scratch the surface of the power that a book can bring you. When you are the author of your own book, the sky is truly the limit.

What you've learned applies universally. Whether you choose to self-publish, seek a traditional publisher, or choose a company like ours these principles will work for you.

Marketing is about positioning yourself favorably in the eyes of your prospects and customers. People like to work wtih experts. And in our society, experts have books. Now you can too.

At Paperback Expert, we specialize in helping small business owners position themselves as *the* expert in their market by becoming an author. Our all-inclusive process takes less than 24 hours of your time, comes with a complete done-for-you marketing system and gives you access to on-going training, coaching and mastermind groups.

Our desire is to help you grow your business and live the life of your dreams. If you are interested in becoming the go-to expert in your area and realizing the dream of being the author of your own book, let us know. We'd love to talk with you.

Position Yourself to Profit,

Michael

Summary: Never Write a Book

When you become an author, you place yourself in a category of one. You gain instant credibility and status, create an endless flow of new leads, and cause prospects to proactively seek you out. If you want to grow your business, you should publish your own book.

Now that you have read *10 ways to Grow Your Business With Your Own Book*, you hopefully agree with everything in that last paragraph. The question is, How? How can you get a book and then use it to grow your business? Who even has the time?!?

We know how you feel. Here at Paperback Expert, there are always more tasks than time to complete them—and you probably feel the same way about your own small business. That's why we've made publishing your own book fast and easy: it takes less than 24 hours of your time and we take care of all the hard parts.

When you follow our 4-Step Process, you won't believe how easy it is to become an author and position yourself as the expert in your market.

The key? Never *write* a book.

Prepare

Determining what to say in your book (and what to leave un-said) could be an overwhelming task if you followed a more traditional approach. We help you think through the content of your book using a simple phone call.

During your Book Outline Call our team works with you to hone your message, helping you think through the "big rocks" that prospects need to understand. We ask questions and reveal stories and anecdotes you use every day as you talk about your business. It's our job to weave your knowledge and stories through the pages of your book in a way that causes people to bond with you emotionally so you can build trust more easily.

By the end of this phone call, together, we'll have created a compelling outline that we'll use as a road map to create the content for your book.

Our unique "Speak-to-Write" process was created so you don't have to spend very much time at all preparing to create your book. You already know what you'd like to say, we simply help you say it in a clear and cohesive way.

Your book will be a key component in your marketing tool chest. We'll help you prepare well so your book will be everything you've dreamed.

Produce

Writing a book isn't so hard—except for the writing part. That's why we created our proprietary "Speak-to-Write" process. Using this process, you can become an author and still *never* write a book.

Designed specifically for the hectic lifestyle of professionals and business owners, our system allows you to speak your book into existence in less than 24 hours of your time. You can talk about your business all day; we help you to quickly and easily get your thoughts out of your head and onto paper by allowing you to talk about your business.

Through a series of phone calls, our team works with you to create the content of your book and craft it into a compelling message in less than 24 hours of your time. Now, it does take a few months to finish the formatting, editing and graphics needed to complete your book, but by following our system, you can create your book in less than 24 hours of your time.

After you "Speak-to-Write" your book, we'll transcribe your message word for word. Then our experienced team formats and edits your manuscript so your message is clear and your book is easy to read. When the first draft is complete, you'll review it for accuracy and be able to make any corrections.

In a separate call, members of our graphics team talk with you to find the right title and create a great looking cover for your book. Branding your book using your current marketing strategy is important as you seek to communicate a consistent message and enhance the trust you'll be creating with prospects and referrals.

We know this will be a time full of excitement and many questions. You can expect regular communication as we guide you through the entire process. After you produce the content of your book, your main concern is to run your business; we'll handle everything else to make your book ready to publish.

Publish

Now that your manuscript is ready and your cover is designed, you are ready to become a published author. Congratulations!

You book will be published in both print and electronic versions. This gives you the greatest flexibility and distribution possible.

Printing is performed in a facility dedicated to high quality and timely turn-around. You don't want to wait months for your book to come off the press, so we keep an eye on the time and can normally have your book quality checked, printed, bound, and delivered in less than 21 days from the day the order is placed.

Getting your book listed on Amazon and converted for the Kindle platform is not as simple as clicking an "upload" button. There are a number of formatting issues that need to be performed to ensure that it is created properly and can be viewed on mobile devices. Our seasoned team of publishing experts know all of the intricacies of this process and can have your ebook ready to publish right on time. Just imagine the thrill of seeing your book on Amazon and Kindle.

Becoming an author used to be out of reach. Today, that's no longer the case. Our system removes all the hurdles and keeps you in control of the content, the rights and the profits.

Now that your book is published, the next step it to promote your book to grow your business.

Promote

You are now an Author. Congratulations!

Your next step is to promote your book (and yourself). You'll find that being an author puts you in a unique position and makes it easy to build trust and grow your business. People perceive authors as experts and authorities. They'll seek you out for advice and listen to your counsel more readily.

There are a variety of ways to use your book to increase your business. You can use your book to:

- Attract new customers by giving your book to them.
- Engage current customers to help them more fully understand your values, background and standards.
- Retain existing customers by gifting a copy of your book to them as a way to say "Thank You!"
- Stimulate referrals more easily by giving a copy (or two) of your book to your satisfied customers as a conversation starter with their friends.

Your book is your best marketing tool. It's like having a conversation with your prospect, but you don't have to be there. They'll easily "hear" your heart since you created your book using the same language you'd use if they were talking with you face to face. That's one reason your book easily helps you build trust.

Your book will become the cornerstone of your marketing efforts. You'll soon become known as "the person who wrote the book" on your topic; and that is a great position to occupy.

When your book is published, we'll continue to provide you with ideas, tools and strategies you can integrate into your marketing plan to leverage your book for all it's worth. You'll be able to connect with other authors and learn how they're using their book to grow their business, and you'll find proven methods to generate more leads, convert more prospects and grow your business.

Creating your own book is no longer out of reach when you follow this 4-Step Process to complete your book in less than 24 hours, then use it to establish client relationships and grow your business.

We help busy people who want to become authors yet never write a book.

If that's you, let us know and we'll schedule a time to talk.

SECTION 3

ON MARKETING

Chapter 6

Your Two Options

In business, you have two options:

Take Your Chances Playing Advertising Roulette

 **Or**

Strategically Aim for the Marketing Bull's Eye

In the next few minutes you're going to learn that marketing doesn't have to be a gamble. When you apply these proven strategies, you can put the odds in your favor and win this game more often than you lose.

I want you to win! So in the following pages, I've laid out for you proven strategies that you can use regardless of the type of business you are in. You're going to learn what it takes to grow your business more rapidly than you ever thought possible. So open your mind as you turn the pages and look for ways to apply what you read to your business. You can experience rapid growth when you focus *On Marketing*.

Chapter 7

Introduction

This is designed to be a reference book. My hope is that you won't read it once and put it on a shelf. I hope it will become a constant companion to remind you of what it takes to grow your business.

When we meet, I'd love nothing more than for you to tell me that you have every page highlighted, dog-eared and underlined. And that this book has helped you break free from the bondage and waste of traditional marketing methods and has been a catalyst for explosive business growth.

As I talk with business people I hear a consistent theme. They know they have to advertise, but they aren't sure how to make it work. I think it was J.C Penney who said:

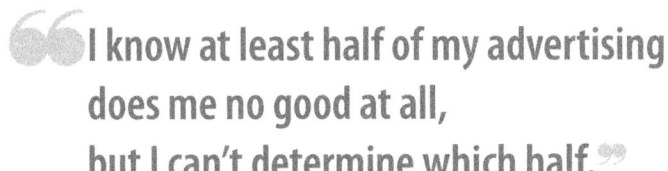

I know at least half of my advertising does me no good at all, but I can't determine which half.

And for some unknown reason, media companies, advertising agencies and business owners have accepted this as truth and wear this as a badge of honor.

I think that's foolish!

And in this book I'm going to explain why.

Chapter 8

What Marketing Is (and Isn't)

Ask 20 people what marketing is and you'll get 20 different answers. No one seems to be able to come to a definitive definition. In less than 3 minutes I was able to find these definitions of marketing from online sources:

The total of activities involved in the transfer of good from the producer or seller to the consumer or buyer, including advertising, shipping, storing and selling.

— Dictionary.com

Marketing is "the activity, set of institutions, and processes for creating, communicating, delivering, and exchanging offerings that have value for customers, clients, partners, and society at large."

— Wikipedia

"Marketing is not the art of finding clever ways to dispose of what you make. It is the art of creating genuine customer value."

— Philip Kotler

Marketing is any contact that your business has with anyone who isn't a part of your business. Marketing is also the truth made fascinating. Marketing is the art of getting people to change their minds.

— Jay Conrad Levinson

"Marketing is getting someone who has a need to know, like and trust you."

— *Jon Jantsch (of Duct Tape Marketing)*

"Marketing is the process of anticipating, managing, and satisfying the demand for products, service and ideas."

— *Wharton School, University of Pennsylvania*

Very little consensus here, wouldn't you agree? And these are some of the "experts" that business people are following. They're all pointing in the same direction, but no one has a definition that you can grab onto, remember easily and quickly judge what you are doing against it.

Now hear me... I too follow some of these people. I'm not bashing them. I believe in what they teach. The point I'm trying to make is that "marketing" is difficult to define. And if you don't have a clear definition when it comes to marketing, you're not going to have the proper focus you need to make things happen. You're going to get frustrated with poor results. Your business is going to be stagnant and you're going to be at the mercy of an ever-changing marketplace and your profits are going to plummet.

This brings much stress into running a business; stress that can be avoided.

This is what drove me to create my own definition of marketing:

Marketing is Everything You Do to GAIN and RETAIN a Customer.

Now that's a pretty simple definition. It's also a very *Holistic* definition.

I believe that your marketing should be holistic. Which

means that it should encompass *every aspect* of your business.

It's definitely NOT isolated to the world of "advertising" to the outside world (more on this later). It literally is **everything you do.** From the ads that you run, to the look, feel & functionality of your website, to how your phones are answered, to the hours your business is open, to how you dress and the policies you have, to the guarantees you offer, to how you follow up with customers before, during and after the sale.

Too often business people take a myopic view of their "marketing" and by doing so drastically limit their effectiveness, reach and profits.

To grow your business, serve more customers and increase your profits you must understand that:

Marketing is Everything You Do to GAIN and RETAIN a Customer.

Nothing less will do.

Chapter 9

7 SMART Ideas

I like to work smart. And I like my marketing to *be* SMART. SMART is an acronym I use for:

Strategic
Measurable
Automated
Response-Oriented
Tactical

If your marketing isn't SMART then you are wasting a lot of your hard earned money. The strategies you'll learn here will help you create a SMART Marketing Plan for your business.

Underlying everything I do are these fundamental ideas. For our purposes here, we'll call them the 7 SMART Ideas:

1. Marketing Is a Battle of Positioning That Is Fought in the Mind of the Customer

   You want to be the 1st person people think of when your product category is mentioned.

2. Choose Your Customer Wisely

   You don't need to sell to everybody. In fact, that's a recipe for failure. The more selective you can be, the more growth you will experience.

3. Position Yourself Purposefully

You have to stand for something or you will fall for anything. What is it that makes you different? How will you stand out from the crowd? Your positioning is critical.

4. Words Are the Greatest Creative Force

When God created the world He spoke it into existence. For you to create massive business growth, you too will need to use words. Images and Logos are helpful, but words are what cause people to take *action*.

5. Know What Your Customer Is Actually Paying For

People don't care about you or your product. They care about themselves and what your product can do for them. Speak to this and your business will grow.

6. Marketing is a Process, Not an Event

Sporadic marketing is a waste of time and money. You need a plan if you're going to grow your business and achieve your dreams and goals. The more consistent you are in your marketing, the greater growth you will experience.

Marketing effects take place over time. Have the patience to be consistent.

7. You Are in the Attraction Business

I don't know what business you *think* you are in, but you are really in the Attraction Business. The day you stop attracting new customers is the day you begin to die.

Chapter 10

The Marketing Audit

When clients retain me to help them grow their business, the fist step is to complete a Marketing Audit. This is a full-day offsite retreat where we analyze your business from every angle, ask penetrating questions, reveal hidden opportunities and begin to create a strategic plan for moving forward to help you achieve your goals.

For our purposes here, I've created a Marketing Audit Snap Shot that you can take. This will reveal how you are doing in 11 different areas. Then, as you continue reading, you'll gain insight into each of these areas and find strategies you can implement to begin growing your business.

Answer each of these questions honestly. Then bookmark this page as you'll want to come back here often.

1. On a scale of 1–10, how important is it for you to attract new customers on a regular basis?

1   2   3   4   5   6   7   8   9   10

2. Do you have in place a reliable system for attracting new customers and identifying where they came from and how they heard about you?

❏ Yes   ❏ No

3. How often do you use a tracking device in your marketing?

❑ Never ❑ Sometimes ❑ Regularly ❑ Always

4. Is your customer engagement process written down, followed and monitored to ensure it is being executed properly by every member of your Team?

❑ Yes ❑ No

5. Do you have a system to reward customers for purchases?

❑ Yes ❑ No

6. Do you have a method that you use regularly to increase the number of repeat purchases?

❑ Yes ❑ No

7. How many referrals do your customers bring you on a monthly basis?

❑ None ❑ 1–5 ❑ 6–10 ❑ 10–20 ❑ More than 20

8. What percentage of your business is from:

Repeat Customers: _____ %

Referrals: _____ %

New Customers: _____ %

9. Do you have a clear, consistent and compelling message that speaks to what your customer really desires to receive from your product/service/offering?

☐ Yes   ☐ No

If "Yes", what is it?

_____

_____

10. How much time do you invest each month working on your marketing?

< 1 Hour   1–3 Hours   4–8 Hours   > 8 Hours

11. How much time do you invest each month thinking about and planning for your business growth?

< 1 Hour   1–3 Hours   4–8 Hours   > 8 Hours

To get from where you are to where you want to be, the first step is giving honest answers to The Marketing Audit. With these answers, and a desire for more, you are now ready to turn your focus to the subject everyone desires but only few achieve…

Chapter 11

The Key to Market Domination

Nike. Coca-Cola. FedEx. Apple. Amazon. eBay. Geico. The list could go on and on. Leaders one and all. But HOW did they get to the top? What caused them to break through the clutter, claim the #1 spot, and stay there?

In a word: **Positioning**.

To be successful – to DOMINATE your market – you have to be in touch with reality. And in marketing, the only reality is in the mind of your customer.

> Marketing is a battle of positioning that's fought in the mind of the customer.

It's not important whether or not you have a better product or service or reputation or warranty. What matters is *HOW* you are positioned in the mind of your customer.

In every customer's head, for every product category, there is a ladder. On each rung of that ladder, there is a product. *Your objective is to occupy the top rung of your product category in the mind of your customer*. That way, whenever your product category is mentioned, they immediately think of YOU!

YOU become the default.

YOU become their go-to source.

YOU become their first and only choice.

THIS is the Position YOU want to have.

It's not always possible to occupy the top rung if somebody else is already there. So when that happens, you have to take a different approach.

That's what Avis had to do.

In the car rental category, Hertz dominated the market for years. Avis and a few others were all vying for 2nd place. That's until someone at Avis came up with an idea....

Instead of attacking Hertz head on and telling people that "We're #1", when everyone knew they weren't, Avis did something very smart. They peered inside the mind of the customer and found a way to become #1.

Avis acknowledged their position as #2 in rental cars. This resonated with people. And then they added a benefit to the customer for choosing Avis:

> **"Avis is only #2 in rent-a-cars,
> so why go with us? We try harder."**

That was a message that resonated in the mind of the customer, could be validated and believed, and that caused people to consider Avis as a viable option.

Do you think it worked???? Like a miracle!

What used to be a fledgling competitor for #2 position suddenly began to gain market share and profits. What caused this sudden growth?

Positioning! It's The Key to Dominating Your Market.

Chapter 12

The 3 Stages of Business

Every business breaks down into the same 3 Stages. I don't care if you are a mom & pop operation or a multi-national conglomerate. At the end of the day all businesses have these same three stages.

The 3 Stages of Business are: Attract | Engage | Retain

Attract

Engage ⟷ Retain

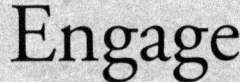 The ATTRACT Stage is where you are attracting prospects and customers TO your business. It encompasses everything from how you are perceived in the marketplace by the customer (think positioning), your reputation, the message that you deliver, the offers you make and even the look of your building and the parking and lighting out front. All of these, and a lot more, are part of your Attract Stage. It's everything you are doing to Attract new customers TO your business.

You need to get customers to run toward you without reservation by offering them something that they want. I liken it to what I call the "Cat & Mouse Game."

Think about having a mouse in your house. You want him gone. You can either get a good cat to chase the mouse all over the place and hope that he eventually catches him; or you can put out some cheese for the mouse and lure him into your trap. Both ways can work, but one is scaring the mouse away and the other is attracting him by giving him what he wants.

You want to Attract customers. The best way to do that is by giving them what they want, not chasing them all over the place.

In the Attract Stage you want to consider what it is that your customer is actually buying from you. Too many times business owners only sell features, or worse yet, they sell by price. You don't want to play that game. Give your customers what they want.

Every year millions of quarter inch drill bits are manufactured and sold. Would you believe that it has been proven that not one person who has purchased one of those drill bits actually wanted to own a drill bit?

The drill bit manufacturer would tell everyone about the quality of their drill bit, the type of steel they use to make their drill bit and the employees who make the drill bit.

All of this falls into the category of "Who cares?"

The customer does not want a drill bit. What the customer wants is a *hole*!

Speak to what it is that your customer is actually paying for and you'll Attract a lot more customers and make a lot more sales.

Engage

So now that you have Attracted a customer, we move into the ENGAGE Stage. This is where your customer begins to connect with you in some way.

It could be that they hear or see your message and go to your website. They might call you. They could even walk through your front door. However they connect with you, that is when the Attract Stage ends and the Engage Stage begins.

NOTE: You must make certain that what you tell them in the Attract Stage matches, or is exceeded by, what they experience in the Engage Stage. Otherwise you'll deliver a bad customer experience and run them away...and they'll take their friends with them.

Haven't we all had the experience of hearing about a new restaurant in town (no offense to restaurant owners)? They talk about how great the food is and their wonderful service. So you go there for dinner only to experience a noisy atmosphere, small portions of adequate food and servers who are too busy doing other things to care for your needs.

How likely are you to return?

How likely are you to tell your friends to go there?

That's what happens when your Attract and Engage Stages are not in sync.

Many of the clients I work with have a pretty good Engage Stage when I meet them. You probably do too. That's because it's what you do. The Engage Stage deals with the operational aspects of your business. It's how you deliver your product or service to your customers. It's the core of your business (from a functional stand point) and it's where you have invested much of your time, effort and resources.

There are always ways to improve your Engage Stage, and a variety of strategies to increase profits in this Stage. You need to become adept at all of these so that you can be certain that you are serving your customers in the best ways, providing for their every desire and doing everything in your power to maximize your average sales volume.

The Engage Stage is a hidden gold mine that many business owners overlook. Don't make that mistake. You need to look carefully at how you Engage with your customers and make certain you are giving them what they really want.

> ## Forget about the drill bit.
> ## Focus on the hole!

Now we come to the Retain Stage. This is where most business owners fail. And that's unfortunate because *the Retain Stage is where wealth is created in a business.* It's where you Retain Customers for Life and gain their Repeat & Referral business.

Retain The Retain Stage is where you are building an on-going relationship with your customer. You are not only sending them "Thank You" notes for their purchase, you are calling them, sending them newsletters, inviting them to special events and giving them special offers and exclusive benefits.

You make them feel special – because they *are* special. They are your customers! They have purchased your product or service. Don't ever allow them to feel like an unloved and un-cared-for orphan.

The Retain Stage can become one of the most profitable stages in your business. *The easiest type of customer to get to purchase from you again is a satisfied customer.* It takes 7-10 times more money to Attract a customer than it does to Retain a customer.

This is the *least* expensive portion of your marketing mix. It's the one where you can have the biggest impact with the least amount of money, because they already know you. And in many cases, you're the incumbent provider of whatever it is you do. It's just a matter of keeping in touch with them and nurturing a life-long relationship with them.

Billions and Billions of dollars are never generated, never realized… simply because of the neglect or

absence of an RETAIN Stage in MOST businesses.

So, look at anything you're doing in your RETAIN Stage, especially in the Nurturing of Life-Long Relationships, as **repeat business insurance**.

That's really what you're doing, isn't it? You're making sure that when they have a need, *they are going to think of you first*, and more often than not, they are going to use you again… and not be tempted to try someone else just because they're being offered a lower price. *You must stay in contact* with them. Repeat business is just the tip of the iceberg in growing your business.

The Retain stage is not only for repeat business, it's also where you gain Referral business. Most business owners are under the illusion that much of their business comes from referrals. What's happening is that they will occasionally have someone come in who says that a friend referred them and the business owners assumes that this is the norm. Most of the time, when you begin tracking where your customers are coming from, referrals are much lower than you think.

There are three types of referrals:

➤ Passive
➤ Reactive
➤ Choreographed

Let's look at each of these in brief so you will have a better idea on how you can take full advantage of your Retain stage by maximizing referrals to grow your business.

Passive referrals are when somebody calls you up and says, "Hey, my brother just used your company and he said I should give you a call."

Passive referrals happen without you doing anything to make them happen.

Reactive referrals are where somebody calls up and says, "Hey, my brother John is thinking about getting a new air conditioner, you should give him a call."

Reactive referrals are where you have to react and do something to make them happen.

Choreographed referrals are where you have trained your customers to notice when a conversation they are having *is about your business category* and to purposefully introduce you into that conversation.

Your customers endorse you and transfer the trust they have in you to their friends.

Choreographed referrals are where your customers notice conversations that are about you and introduce their friends to you.

To grow your business quickly, invest some focused effort on your Retain Stage and you'll begin seeing your profits go straight to the bottom line.

Chapter 13

The Alphabet Maze

The Alphabet Maze

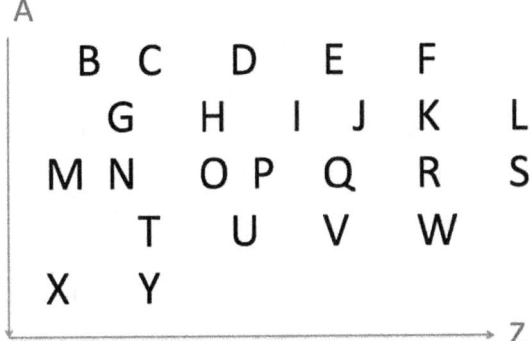

The path that your customer takes on their way to a purchase is what I refer to as The Alphabet Maze.

Every customer has a slightly different path they will take. Some will move fast while others meander more slowly. Whatever their pace, it is YOUR RESPONSIBILITY to lead them through this Maze so that they end up at their (and your) desired location.

Most business people want to take someone from A to Z as quickly as possible. And if the customer "just isn't ready to make a decision today", then we leave them and look for someone else we can help.

That's very short sighted! Always remember that:

"Between A and Z there's a great big B through Y."

A better tactic is to **establish a process** that allows people to come through The Alphabet Maze at their own pace. You will be guiding them the entire way, giving them information, answering their questions, building trust and becoming an advocate. This way, WHEN THEY ARE READY to make a purchase, YOU are their only logical choice.

The Alphabet Maze is part of your ENGAGE Stage. "A" is when they first connect with you in some fashion; "Z" represents the consummation of the sale. To get them into The Maze you first have to ATTRACT them. Then, after the sale you need to RETAIN them. The Alphabet Maze sits right in the middle.

To lead them through this Maze takes some forethought on your part. It can consist of a series of Free Reports or Pre-Written Emails set up in an Auto-Responder System that are sent on a predetermined time frame. You could also include your Free Recorded Message as part of this process. You may even invite them to a special VIP event.

At this stage you are wooing their business. Building trust. Establishing yourself as THE SOURCE and THE SOLUTION to their needs. YOU are the expert. YOU have what they need. It is up to YOU to win their heart, overcome their concerns, remove any and every barrier to action (more on this later) and assure them – then re-assure them – that they will be completely taken care of and have no risk doing business with you.

The Alphabet Maze is a critical component of your Marketing System. It allows you to maintain a "full funnel" of interested prospects; each moving closer and closer to the point of doing business with you.

By focusing on The Alphabet Maze you will be able to even-out your sporadic cash flow, establish a predictable pace of customer conversion, and learn ways to increase the speed that many move through The Maze. This all adds revenue to your bottom line and allows you to experience consistent business growth.

The Alphabet Maze is an extremely powerful concept that helps you build trust with your prospects so that they become not only clients, but customers for life.

Chapter 14

The Marketing Triad

Any stool worth its weight has 3 legs. Any fewer and it will topple; any more and it will have the potential to rock. Three is the perfect number.

Similarly, your marketing should be founded on three as well, what I call The Marketing Triad.

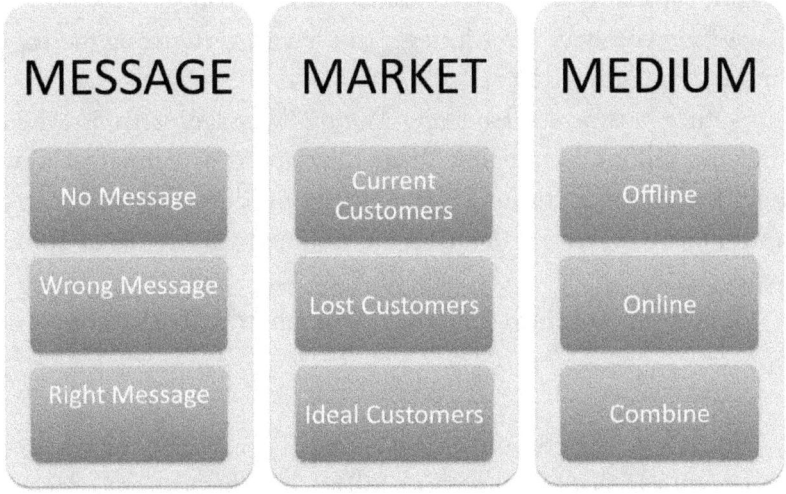

MESSAGE — No Message — Wrong Message — Right Message

MARKET — Current Customers — Lost Customers — Ideal Customers

MEDIUM — Offline — Online — Combine

The three components of every marketing strategy and campaign are your Message, your Market and the Medium you choose.

Too often a businessperson completely ignores the Message, never chooses a specific target Market, and picks a Medium by random selection, because they've always used this one, or due to the presence of a media rep standing in their doorway reminding them of a deadline that's fast approaching. None of these are the right way to market.

MESSAGE

Your MESSAGE is critical. It is the foundation for your Position in the Market (which you'll remember is found in the mind of the customer).

Very seldom do you find a business (local or any other) that has a strong, compelling, benefit oriented Message that they deliver consistently to a specific group of people.

Most businesses have No Message at all. Their marketing is nothing more than Name, Rank and Serial Number. Price is the only thing they have to offer. This is a BAD PLACE to be. What this tells the customer is that you have nothing else to offer. You *are* just like everyone else (just as I've suspected) and there's **no reason** for me to choose to do business with you.

When you have No Message, you have a very strong message in the wrong direction.

Other businesses have the Wrong Message. This is when they are talking about how great they are as a company. How long they've been around. The lines of product that they carry and their wonderful staff that has combined experience of 1,000 years.

All of this falls into the category of what??? That's right:

Who Cares???!!!!

I hate to be the one who has to tell you this (not really, I believe this is part of my responsibility), but the customer doesn't care about you, your products or your employees. The customer is only interested in what your product or service will do for them.

They don't buy your products for its features. They buy for the benefits they will receive from owning.

Remember this:

No one wants to be sold. Everyone loves to buy.

Speak in terms of what owning your product/service will do for them. Paint a picture that they'll not only remember, but also desire. We call it "future pacing." It's allowing them to envision what life will be like when they own your product/service, and how great everything will be.

No, this is not manipulation! That only occurs when you don't deliver what you promise. You had better never do that!

Future Pacing is bringing the desired benefits of future ownership into the present through carefully crafted words, pictures and mental images. It's a craft that you should work on and master if you want to become a Master Marketer.

You need to invest some time crafting the Right Message. This is a Message that is ALL about your customer.

Saying the right thing is the first part of developing your positioning and differentiating yourself in the marketplace. And it's the second most important part of creating a marketing strategy that results in rapid customer attraction and sustainable business growth.

MARKET The most important component in developing your marketing plan is to say the right message *to* the right market.

We call this the Message to Market Match.

The reason this is THE MOST IMPORTANT is that you can say the Right Thing, but if you are saying it to the WRONG person, your results are going to be less than you desire.

Consider advertising the benefits of your 24/7 plumbing service that comes with a 30 minute on-site response time and a 100% risk free guarantee at the normal day rates, but sending this to those living in an apartment complex.

Absurd, you say??? Similar things happen most every day.

When you take your message and simply blast it out through traditional media channels (radio, newspaper, outdoor, magazines, cable/tv, etc.) this is precisely what you are doing.

Can you get some response doing this? Yes. Could you get an even better response by carefully choosing a target market that is "hungry" for what you offer? Absolutely. Is this much more difficult to do? Not at all. In fact, it's not that complex at all, once you know how to do it.

The Market component of The Marketing Triad breaks your "market" down into 3 buckets:

Current Customers, Lost Customers & Ideal Customers.

These are just the start, but when you focus on these three, you'll find that you'll get a much faster (and larger) ROI on your marketing efforts.

You should never neglect to market to your current customers. Just because they are buying from you now, doesn't mean that they won't buy even more from you if you give them the opportunity (and it helps to insulate them from being wooed by a competitor).

Your current customers are your best source for increased income. They already Know, Like & Trust you. Your job is to give them even more reasons to buy more from you and offer them other buying options that they'd never expect you to offer.

There's an entire process called Joint Venture Marketing that we don't have time for here, but suffice it to say, that when you learn how to structure and execute a Joint Venture that adds value to your current customers, your profits will increase and your customer retention will be much higher.

Lost customers pose another great opportunity for business growth. That's because there are only about *6 reasons people stop doing business with you*, and many of those can be overcome.

Here are the top reasons people stop doing business with you:

- 68% upset with the treatment they've received
- 14% dissatisfied with product or service
- 9% begin doing business with a competitor
- 5% seek alternatives or develop other business relationships

- 3% move away
- 1% die

96% of your Lost Customers are still buying what you sell. They're just buying it from someone else.

Research has proven that you can get back up to 26% of your Lost Customers if you have a plan and a process for doing so. I call it a *Customer Reactivation Campaign* and it's one of the easiest ways to increase your profits quickly.

Now we move on to Ideal Customers. This is where the BIG MONEY is! You need to know a couple of things if you're going to grow your business:

1. What is the Lifetime Value of Your Customer?
2. Who is Your Ideal Customer?

The answers to these two questions will help you target your Message to the Right Market more rapidly.

Knowing the Lifetime Value (LTV) of a Customer is a critical number because it affects how you look at every part of your business and marketing. Here's a simple way to calculate this number for your business:

Average Amount of a Purchase $ _____

Average # of Purchases / year _____

Average # of years you serve a customer _____

Multiply these numbers together and you'll have the Lifetime Value of your Average Customer. For Example:

$150 Average Purchase
X 3 Purchases per year
X 8 Years of purchasing
= $3,600 as the Lifetime Value of a Customer.

Now you know that every new customer you attract is worth NOT $150 (the initial sale), but $3,600 (their LTV), THAT will change the way you treat them from the very start!

It also impacts how much you are able to invest to attract new customers. The setting of your ad budget is not something most business people are taught how to do properly. Normally you'll follow industry standards, or heaven forbid, the advice of your CPA (nothing against CPAs – I just believe we should all stay within our area of expertise).

When you know the LTV of your customer, then you can begin looking at WHO your Ideal customer is based on the information you have, or can find out, about them, including (but not limited to):

> geographic
> demographic
> psychographic

Gathering this data isn't as difficult as you might think, and you probably have, or know, much of it right now. What you need to do is assemble it in an organized fashion and use it to more accurately target your Ideal Customers who are not currently doing business with you.

There's a phrase I learned that you should commit to memory and vow to live by if you are serious about growing your business to new levels. I originally heard this concept from my mentor, Dan Kennedy:

"WHO Controls Your Income!"

Meaning: Who you attract and choose to do business with is more determinative of your future income than most anything else. If you attract poor people, you'll have a poor income. If you attract the wealthy, you'll have a better income. If you attract the super-rich, you'll never have to worry about money again.

So WHO are you attracting today?

WHO do you want to attract in the future?

It's a very simple question that has extremely profound implications for your marketing and your business.

Determine WHO your Ideal Customer is, know their Lifetime Value and use this information to make better decisions that will put more money in your bank each and every month.

So we've talked about the importance of your Message. You now understand the different components of your Market. The final part of The Marketing Triad is the Medium that you will use.

MEDIUM At its very basic level, the Medium is the Delivery Method. It's the vehicle that you will use to get your Message to your Market. At the ground level, there is OFFLINE Media and ONLINE Media.

OFFLINE is what we refer to as "traditional" media: Newspaper, Radio, Outdoor, Direct Mail, Magazines, TV, Cable, etc.

ONLINE encompasses: Websites, Email, Blogs, Social Media Platforms, Podcast, Videos, etc.

A very common approach is to chase the New at the expense of the Old. Business owners far and wide are hypnotized by the next new "shiny object" that appears as their Prince Charming who's going to ride into town and save them from all of their idiotic marketing mishaps.

They hear about the newest whatever and spend time, energy and money chasing it, dabbling in it, and getting distracted by it. All the while their business is falling off because they are no longer giving any attention to the one who "brought them to the dance."

Hear me now: I'm all in favor of online media. And I am passionate about offline media. I just think a better approach is to bring them together in what I call, COMBINE Media.

The more you can use multiple platforms to convey your Message to your Market using a variety of Media the better you will be.

However—and this is A BIG HOWEVER—you need to fully understand this principle of marketing:

NEVER, NEVER, NEVER...

buy a bigger media provider

than you can afford to be a BIG PLAYER on.

As Marketing Consultant and Author Roy Williams says,

There is No Future Being a Small Fish in a Big Pond.

It is much more productive, not to mention more profitable, to be a Big Fish in a Small Pond. That way everyone knows who *you* are. And when they know who you are, they're more likely to do business with you.

One way to do this is by joining a service club or a lead passing group and working to be one of the leaders, like the President. Everyone in the group knows who the President is, even if the President doesn't know who they are. You want to do the same thing with your marketing.

You want to win the hearts of a group of people and become *their* WHO.

It's not that difficult. It takes patience, focus and guts. Most of which (for some unknown reason) the typical business owner lacks. Fortunately, you are not one of them. You are willing to go against what "they" say and do what has been proven to work for decades. You are committed to business growth; to doing the smart thing, to doing what it takes to make things happen.

Now you know the importance of crafting the Right Message, targeting the Right Market and using the Right Medium so that your own Marketing Triad will produce measureable results.

But all of this will fail unless you understand this next concept, which fewer than 1 in 100 business owners have ever heard about.

Chapter 15

The 3 Worlds of Business

Have you ever been in a situation where a decision has been handed to you and your response was, "Where in the world did *that* idea come from?"

Well, you're about to find out.

According to Roy Williams, there are three worlds that govern all of your business life:

- ➤ The World Outside Your Door
- ➤ The World Inside Your Door
- ➤ The World of the Executive Office

These 3 Worlds impact your business growth more than you may realize.

The World Outside Your Door is the World of Public Perception. It's the world of reputation, word-of-mouth and image. This is the world where referrals happen... or don't. It's where people talk about you when you are not present. It's a vibrant world that never sleeps. What you do to influence this world can make or break your company.

The World Inside Your Door is the World of Customer Experience. This world encompasses everything from your parking lot and lighting, to your entry way, to what they see, smell and feel as they enter your lobby, to how they are greeted, to the pictures on the wall and the coffee and beverages that you serve. It's how your staff cares for them and how well their experience is choreographed to make them feel comfortable. It is, many times, the "make it or break it" world for your customers. It is here that many customers experience a "disconnect" from the Attract Stage to the Engage Stage.

If what you promised them in the Attract Stage is not readily experienced here, they will leave to never come back. And, most of the time, they'll tell many of their friends who live in the World Outside Your Door.

You must do everything you can to maximize, control and choreograph every detail of the Customer Experience. By doing so you will increase your sales (both today and in the future) and influence positively the "word of mouth" that happens outside your door.

Both of these worlds are determined by the decisions you make in **The World of the Executive Office**.

This is the world that you – the business owner – occupy. It's where you make decisions that impact each of the other two worlds. From the products that you carry, to the hours you are open, to the people you employ, to the policies you create. Every little detail and decision you make impacts the other two worlds positively or negatively.

How much time do you invest in the World of the Executive Office each week?

How much time do you really invest working ON your business vs. working IN your business? A great book to read on this topic (though he doesn't call it by these names) is *The E-Myth* by Michael Gerber.

Invest some time understanding these 3 Worlds and you'll never again hear someone remark about one of your decisions by screaming: "Where in the world did *that* idea come from?"

Chapter 16

5 Pillars of Business Growth

What is the difference between a Diving Board and the Parthenon?

It's the number of Pillars holding them up.

As a business growth consultant, my job is to assess your business and help you build multiple pillars of revenue. By doing this, you immediately begin to level out your income fluctuations and you put yourself on a trajectory to higher and higher profits. There is no limit to the number of pillars you can build into your business.

Following are The 5 Pillars of Business Growth.

Chapter 17

Pillar 1: Three Ways to Grow a Business

> Increase the # of Customers (Attract)
> Increase the Avg. $/sale (Engage)
> Increase the # of Repeat & Referral Sales (Retain)

No matter what you want to do or make happen, these are the only 3 ways to grow your business. It's really refreshing when you think about it. Putting everything into a very simple matrix like this brings instant clarity and ease of communication.

Understand that out of everything you've ever learned or any new "shiny object" that appears, it all comes down to the fact that you only have 3 Ways to Grow a Business.

Chapter 18

Pillar 2: Two Ways to See

Tunnel Vision

Most business people get caught in "Tunnel Vision."

This is where you are myopically focused on your business, your industry and your competition. Your advertising and marketing looks pretty much like everyone else's.

Additionally, your advertising budget and business growth numbers are similar to theirs. In fact, you base your "success" on how closely you can match industry averages.

This, my friend, is a recipe for disaster! What you need is a new perspective.

You need a new way to view the world. Some fresh ideas and a method for seeing in a whole new light.

What you need is…

Funnel Vision

Funnel Vision is a way of seeing the world where you look *outside* of your industry for proven ideas and concepts that are producing results. You then find ways to adapt those concepts to your business.

Without fail they will work! Believe me, if something is working in one industry, there's a way to make it work in another.

Where do you think the fast food industry got the idea for the drive through window? From the banking industry.

What about the dry cleaner who picks up and delivers your clothes to your house? From the pizza delivery business.

And where do you think Omaha Steaks learned that they could effectively sell food directly to the consumer, bypassing the grocery store? The direct mail catalogue industry.

All of these examples were not being done at one time. It

took someone with Funnel Vision to see something working in a different industry than their own, ponder HOW it might work in their business, and then ACT on that idea and give it a try.

That, my friend, is how fortunes are made. You need a fresh perspective to find new pathways to profit. You won't find them by looking within your industry. They are easily found by simply being observant and looking around you.

Notice your surroundings. Ask questions. Consider alternatives. You'll be amazed at the ideas you come up with. Don't discount an idea just because no one else in your industry is doing it. That's precisely the type of idea you need to chew on.

Developing Funnel Vision isn't difficult, but it does take practice. Begin today by noticing some of the advertisements that are around you right now. Find something you like about an advertisement (that may be difficult at times) and then ask yourself how you could apply that to your business. Or the next time you're watching an infomercial or a video online, try to discern their formula and why they are doing what they are doing. How does it make you feel? What are they saying? Then consider how you could apply some of those concepts to your own marketing.

We call this Modeling. You are not stealing or plagiarizing anything. You are finding a proven model, modifying it to fit your business, then deploying it in a similar manner.

You've heard the old adage, "Don't reinvent the wheel." That's the foundational belief behind modeling. Without question, modeling is one of the fastest ways to grow your business. It begins when you lose your Tunnel Vision and begin seeing with Funnel Vision.

Chapter 19

Pillar 3: One Unique Message

Everyone has a story to tell. How clearly are you telling yours? By developing your 1 Unique Message – what we call your Unique Selling Proposition (USP) – you will instantly separate yourself from everyone else. Here are a few examples, see if you can name the companies:

Fresh, Hot Pizza Delivered in 30 Minutes, Guaranteed.

When it absolutely, positively has to be there overnight.

The World's Largest Bookstore

How'd you do? If you answered "Domino's Pizza", "FedEx" and "Amazon.com" you did well.

Each of these is Unique to that company, allows them to OWN a Position in the mind (remember Positioning?) and communicates a Benefit to their Market.

Sometimes your USP can be in more of a story form, like TOMS Shoes or Tom Bodett of Motel 6 fame.

Normally, it's better to be succinct, direct and memorable, especially for small businesses that don't have a 7-figure ad budget.

You need to determine your USP and use it as the headline for your ads, the banner on your website and the lead on your business card. So how do you do this?

Here are three simple steps to crafting your USP:

1. Narrowly define your Positioning

2. Be as Specific as possible

3. Add a Guarantee

Domino's didn't say they had *good* pizza. They said it would be "fresh and hot." *That* they could deliver on!

Fresh, Hot Pizza
Delivered in 30 Minutes, Guaranteed.

They made it specific by saying, "delivered in 30 minutes". And they backed it up with, "Guaranteed!"

Model your USP after Domino's and you'll be in good company.

Chapter 20

Pillar 4: Remove the Barriers to Action

What's keeping your customers from taking action? Barriers can be physical, financial or emotional.

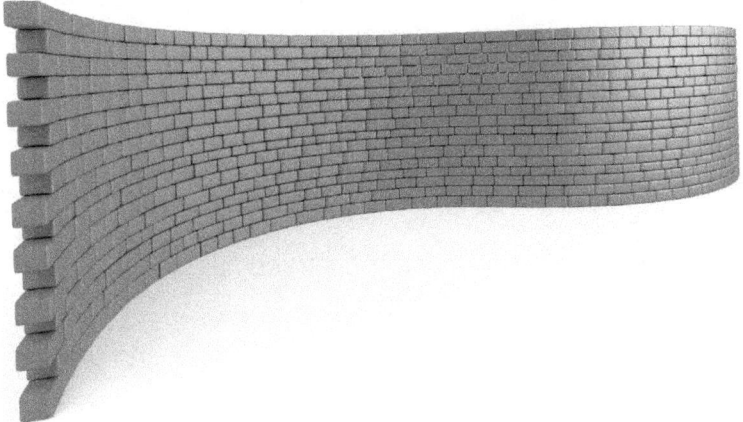

The most common barriers are the objections you get from your prospects. You need to remove the reasons they give for not taking action now—their barriers to action—so you can make more sales, satisfy more customers, and grow your business.

In order to remove barriers you first need to identify them. I recommend that you gather your team and write down *every* objection, concern, stall tactic and reason they have heard for not buying. Put each one on a separate 3X5 card. Prioritize them by their importance to your customer (this should be obvious as they will be the most popular answers). Then organize them in order.

Make sure you get them all. Don't settle for the top two or three. Your list will probably be a dozen or so by the time you are done.

Now you need to begin working on ways to eliminate every one of those barriers. By being proactive here, you'll eliminate the stalls that happen at the time of the close because you will actually be bringing them up earlier in the Engagement Stage, educating your customer, and establishing a safety net of comfort for them by removing all fear and anxiety from the transaction.

This you will do by implementing one of the easiest, yet most often overlooked, barrier removal strategies that successful businesspeople have been using for decades.

A 100% Risk Free Guarantee is one of the easiest ways to remove barriers and increase sales at the same time. It's so simple, yet few people use it.

Let me ask you a few questions:

1. Do you believe in your product or service?

2. Do you want your customers to be happy?

3. If they aren't satisfied with their purchase, and they ask for a refund, would you give it to them?

Assuming you've answered "yes" to these questions, then why would you not take that guarantee and, instead of hiding it in the fine print or never mentioning it for fear that someone might take you up on it, why don't you blatantly announce it to the world and stake your reputation on it. You could even use this as part of your Unique Selling Proposition like Domino's did.

They guaranteed to deliver a fresh, hot pizza to you in 30 minutes or less or it was free. Do you think they bought a few pizzas over the years? I'm sure they did. But, instead of costing them money, it actually worked in their favor because their customers knew that they stood behind what they said. This builds more trust and greater customer loyalty.

The percentage of people who will ever take you up on a risk free guarantee is so small that the increased profits more than cover it. It's not even a factor.

Not to mention how much more growth you're going to have since you are boldly stating your position and giving people a reason to choose you because of what you stand for. *You can successfully remove most every barrier to entry by carefully crafting a risk free guarantee and stating it boldly.*

One of my clients is an auto repair shop. They've been around for over 15 years and have a good reputation. So when we wanted to break into a new Market, we knew we needed a strong positioning statement (a Message) that would hit the bull's eye with our target market.

We discussed different options based on the research we had obtained related to the pain points of our target (remember that people will do more to avoid pain than pursue pleasure). These people weren't getting good service from the dealer, and it took many days to get their vehicle in and out of the shop. They also would have to call back every day or so to hear what was happening with their repair.

So, we considered our options and landed on this positioning statement and Risk-Free Guarantee…

The 4-Hour or Free Guarantee

We'll call you within four hours of your appointment with an update on your vehicle or we'll repair it for FREE!

Now that's a pretty bold statement. No one in his industry or his market was doing anything like this.

So we launched this with a 5-step direct mail campaign aimed at our specific target market, put it on our website and even created a 24/7 Free Recorded Message to further explain and reinforce our position.

In other words, we weren't hiding it. You shouldn't either. When you remove the Barriers to Action you'll make a lot more sales and your business will grow.

Chapter 21

Pillar 5: Develop Customers for Life

Wealth in business is created here.

Once you know the Lifetime Value of your Customer you begin to understand how important it is to keep your customers coming back. And when you recall the 6 reasons people stop doing business with you, and how easy most of them are to overcome, you start to wonder why more business people don't focus on the Retain Stage.

It seems that most businesses are content with Attracting customers and Engaging them for a simple transaction. Retaining them for future purchases doesn't seem to enter their mind. After reading this chapter, you'll never allow that to happen to you.

I first learned this concept from a book written by Carl Sewell. Carl is a Cadillac dealer in Texas (one of the nation's largest and most profitable) who realized one day the Lifetime Value of his customers and decided right then and there that he wanted customers for life.

Carl then recreated his entire business to achieve this one objective. Everything Sewell Cadillac does is done to retain customers for life. And because of this one decision that Carl made, Sewell Cadillac is legendary in their industry.

You too can develop customers for life. There are a variety of factors you need to consider, and a myriad of ways to cause this to occur. One very simple step you can take right away is to *create and mail a customer newsletter every month*. When I say "mail",

I mean with a postage stamp, not clicking the send button. You can do an email newsletter as well, but nothing – I repeat, *nothing* – *compares to a printed monthly newsletter going out to your current and former customers.*

What better way is there to stay in touch with them, AND to maintain your Top of Mind Awareness (TOMA) with them?

When they stay engaged with you they continue to bond with you. And since so many businesses are getting away from sending things in the mail (stating that email is not only faster, but less expensive – only one of which is actually true) you will definitely stand out. And when you are consistent, you will continue to develop trust with them. And trust is many times the determinative factor in repeat business.

So **make a decision right now** to begin writing your own monthly newsletter and mailing it to your current and past customers. If this seems like an overwhelming task and you'd like some help through a done-for-you customer retention system, there are many companies that can help you. Just search for "done-for-you newsletters."

The other aspect of this is that because you are staying in touch with your current and past customers, they will be much more likely to refer you to their friends, neighbors, relatives and business associates. There are many ways to orchestrate referrals, and having a monthly printed newsletter is only one strategy.

We all know how much more expensive it is to get a customer than to keep a customer. So *decide right now* that you will begin building your business and increasing your profits by developing customers for life.

Those are **The 5 Pillars of Business Growth**.

1. 3 Ways to Grow Your Business

2. 2 Ways to See

3. 1 Unique Message

4. Remove the Barriers to Action

5. Develop Customers for Life

By integrating these five pillars into your marketing, you'll build a stronger foundation and be less vulnerable to market fluctuations. Your profits will increase and your business will grow.

Chapter 22

One Question You Must Answer

So much money is wasted in marketing every day because people don't answer this one simple question.

It's not a difficult question at all. The challenge exists because we are not taught to anticipate this question—therefore, we do not answer this question.

This one question is THE question that every customer is asking himself or herself before taking a step in your direction (think Alphabet Maze) and before they ever buy from you (think Removing the Barriers to Action). It's a question that you must answer convincingly and repeatedly.

The question that every customer is asking that you must answer is simply:

What's In It For Me?

That's really all the customer wants to know. But instead of telling them what's in it for them, most business owners dribble on and on about how great they are (remember the drill bit and the hole????).

Your customer is far too busy to be concerned about you. They are only interested in what your product/service can do for them, and how it can satisfy some of their deepest longings.

Sometimes these longings are needs; sometimes they are desires. Regardless of what they are, if you don't effectively answer this one question, you will lose more sales than you make.

So, how do you answer this question in a way that will ATTRACT customers TO you???

You have to look at what you offer from the perspective of your customer. It takes seeing with AN OUTSIDE-IN approach. Many times, it will take an outside observer whom you can trust.

You see, as the business owner, you are too close to your business to see it as your customer sees it. As the saying goes, "you can't see the forest for the trees."

You are the captain of your own ship, sailing on the seas of commerce. With one hand shadowing the sun from your eyes you look to the horizon plotting your course. Your other hand firmly holds the wheel as you make necessary course corrections so that you arrive at your destination. All seems good until you pull back and realize the fact that:

YOU ARE INSIDE THE BOTTLE
LOOKING OUT TRYING TO SEE YOURSELF.

What you need is a new paradigm. A fresh set of eyes. Someone who will tell you what your customer (or most media reps) never will.

It's almost impossible for you to notice that one of your sails has a rip in it that's beginning to expand. Or that your mast is starting to crack. Or that the morale of your crew is diminishing because the wind has died down and your supplies are being rationed and rumors are beginning to fly.

This only happens in fairy tales and pirate stories, I know. But what IF it's happening in your business right now? How would you know?

When you are so focused on where you are going that you aren't taking care of your team – or your customer – you are in stormy waters.

The fastest way to navigate out of this stormy sea is to answer the one question that your customer is asking:

What's In It For Me?

When your customer asks you a question, it's good for you to answer it. *Your customer is always asking this one question.* Be sure you give them a compelling answer so they will know without question, What's In It For Them!

Chapter 23

Fulcrum Positioning

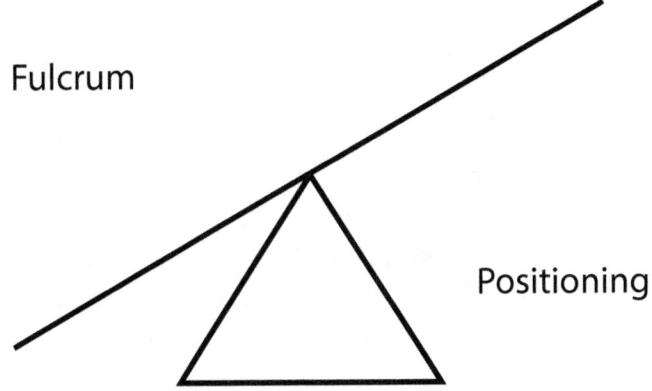

Fulcrum

Positioning

Integrating Strategies for Greater Growth

A fulcrum is the point on which a lever rests or is supported and on which it pivots. In this image, it's where the top of the triangle intersects the lever.

To gain greater leverage in your marketing, which leads to greater growth and more profits, you need to develop methods to reposition the fulcrum so that you can have greater output for the same amount of input.

The simplest fulcrum is a teeter-totter. The fulcrum is in the middle so that the input force exerted on one-end equals the output force on the other. Because it's a balanced system, it will give you a 1:1 ratio. That's why a smaller child has to sit farther back when teetering with a heavier child.

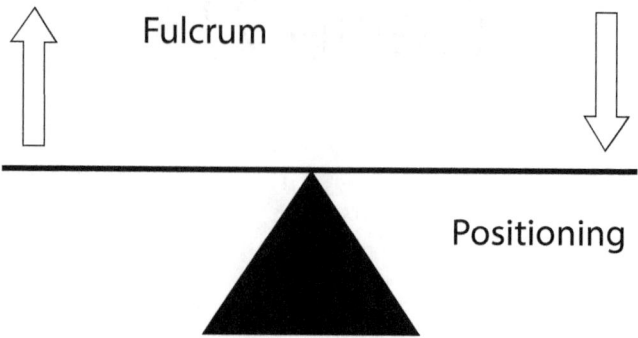

Another way to manipulate this situation is to move the fulcrum (not as easy to do with teeter-totters as it is with your marketing). By relocating the fulcrum, you gain an advantage through the creation of a lever.

And with careful positioning of your fulcrum, and the right lever, you can create a multiplying effect from your marketing.

You are putting IN the same amount of time, energy and money, but you are getting OUT much more in sales, profits and income.

This is such a simple concept, but very few business people apply it. They are like the captain on that ship…too focused on what they are doing to ever consider other ways of growing.

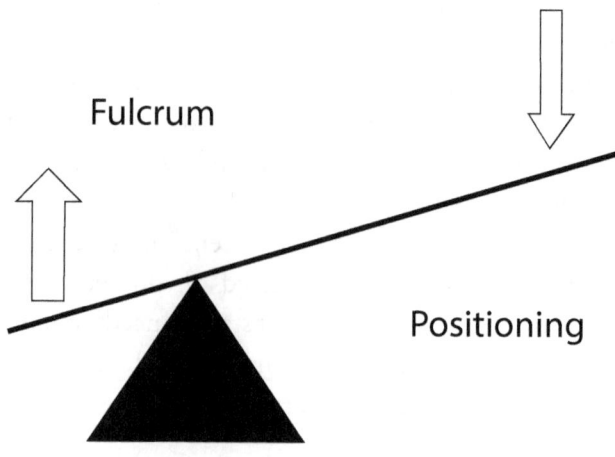

Simply by understanding the concept of Fulcrum Positioning, you will now begin to think of new and different ways to leverage your marketing.

Now don't let the word "leverage" scare you. I'm not talking about going into debt or putting yourself at risk. I'm talking about positioning yourself to maximize your profits by integrating strategies for greater growth.

Too many times you are taught to do one thing at a time. It's called doing things in Sequence.

What you need to do is work on things **Simultaneously** in order to gain more in less time.

Now this isn't multi-tasking; that's been proven not very effective. It *is* working on multiple strategies at the same time that all have one goal in mind: Growth!

Fulcrum Positioning is one of the hidden keys to rapid growth. Successful companies have been using this concept for decades. Business schools don't teach it. Media reps don't know it. Now you understand it. Go, therefore, and apply it to your business.

Running a business isn't child's play, but you can learn a lesson at the playground if you are observant (Funnel Vision). Ponder how many strategies you can integrate to produce greater growth in your business as you apply the concept of Fulcrum Positioning.

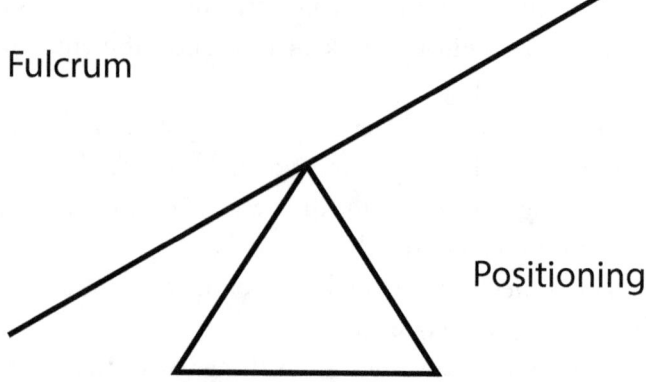

Fulcrum

Positioning

Integrating Strategies for Greater Growth

Chapter 24

The Strategy of FREE

Chris Anderson wrote a book a few years ago titled:

FREE
The Future of a Radical Price

This book is a must-read for anyone who is serious about growing their business. It will definitely rock your world and give you great real-life examples of how many companies are using FREE to increase their bottom line.

Skeptical? Ever hear of Google? How much do they charge you to use their search engine?

What about eBay? Evernote? Craigslist? WordPress?

All very profitable companies using a FREE strategy.

Those are all online companies. But will this work for a normal brick and mortar business?

Consider the classes (and the Genius Bar) inside The Apple Store. Or the ice cream store down the street that gives free cones to kids under 4 (they don't come there by themselves). Or those funny cows at Chick-fil-A giving out free chicken sandwich "coupons" (though they don't call them coupons).

All regular companies, many just like yours, using a FREE strategy to impact the bottom line positively.

Don't get me wrong; I'm *not* in favor of giving away the farm. But *I am in favor* of removing any and every barrier to action and giving my customers a reason to act NOW!

In most cases, FREE is the "magic bullet" that starts the train rolling through The Alphabet Maze. There are so many ways you can use FREE in your marketing that we'll never be able to discuss them here. What I do want to do, however, is to get you thinking outside the box. STOP thinking that your business is different or that FREE only works in the online world. It's Not and it Doesn't!

FREE is a *strategy*. And like every strategy I teach, it has to make sense for you, your customer and what you want to make happen.

Not every strategy will work in every situation, but FREE will work in most. It simply takes a little thought and a fresh perspective. You won't find the answer looking inside of your industry, or even by observing your competition. You'll need to look elsewhere.

The most attractive part of FREE is that it allows you to begin filling the TOP of your Sales Funnel. Developing a Lead Generation System that you can put on autopilot will do more for your business growth than anything else you can imagine (we'll discuss this concept in an upcoming chapter).

When you have a continuous flow of new customers funneling through The Alphabet Maze you can't help but serve more customers, make more sales, increase your income and grow your business. One of the first and foundational parts of this Customer Attraction System is the Strategy of FREE.

What are you going to do with the Strategy of FREE?

How might you apply this to your business?

What do you offer that your customer would love to have? Find a way to give it to them (or at least a portion of it) for FREE!

Experiment with the Strategy of FREE. Nothing has to be long-term or set in concrete. Try it. Modify it. Test it. You'll never know what's possible until you give it a shot.

Begin today—fill the funnel with interested, qualified and pre-disposed prospects that you can turn into paying customers.

It all begins when you use The Strategy of FREE.

Chapter 25

Creating an Automated Sales Force

Recruiting, hiring, training, motivating and retaining a competent sales person is challenging at best. Seems like when you find a good one, they leave. And many times, the ones who stay… well, you know where I'm going.

What if you could create an Automated Sales Force? What if there was a way to put your marketing on autopilot, where you could create it once and let it go—or at least not have to touch it very often. How much time would this save you? How much more money could you make? What would you do with yourself???

Well, this isn't a dream. It's one of the foundational aspects that I teach to my private clients. And since you had the sense to read my book, you are going to get an inside look at how some of the world's most profitable companies create income by using an Automated Sales Force.

There are a variety of ways to generate sales automatically. We'll discuss four of them here:

1. *24/7 Free Recorded Message*

Without question, this is one of THE most under-utilized systems in business. Having a 24/7 Free Recorded Message Hotline should be mandatory for every business. There are so many different ways for you to use this to attract new customers it will boggle your mind.

It's one of the first systems I implement with my private clients. It's really a no-brainer.

People are hesitant to take action. It's human nature. Most ads want you to pick up the phone to call or just come in. What is your prospect thinking??? "No way! I'm not going to do that. I don't want to talk to a sales person. They'll never let me go. I've been down that road before. Not on your life!"

So, to remove this barrier to action, all you need to do is activate this barrier removal system called a 24/7 Free Recorded Message.

Since it's a recorded message, **there's no fear** in calling it. They won't be talking to a live human, and they can call when it's convenient for them. And they'll believe you more than if you tell them the same thing in person. It's as if they think, "If they are willing to say this in a public forum, it must be true." This attitude works to your advantage.

Now for you, this is a great deal because you not only get a toll free number, you also receive 10 different extensions that you can use any way you want. And check this out; when someone calls your Free Recorded Message, you can get a text or email sent to you telling you that they called! How's that for direct response marketing?!

You can use a 24/7 Free Recorded Message to deliver a sales presentation, give directions, announce a special, give a discount, capture information, recruit employees or as a post-sale thank you. The ideas and uses are endless.

We regularly use them in conjunction with print advertising for our private clients. As a call to action, we'll give them a website, our normal phone number, and our 24/7 Free Recorded Message. You'll be pleasantly surprised at how many prospects become customers when you use a free-recorded message. It's so very simple to use and you can be set up in under 15 minutes.

2. *Customer Attraction Systems*

Most companies have one or two ways that they attract customers. World-class companies have dozens. One of the paradigm shifts you need to make is to understand what business you are really in.

Regardless of what you sell:

You Are In The ATTRACTION Business!

Attracting New Customers is the life-blood of your business. You can never leave that to chance. Nor can you only have one method of doing this (remember the diving board and the Parthenon examples?).

Developing a variety of Customer Attraction Systems that you can implement and have operating simultaneously is one way to move the fulcrum in your favor. These don't have to be complex or complicated systems. They simply need to be strategic and integrated.

For example, one system could look like this. You create a Free Report that answers the 1 question your prospect/customer is asking (do you remember what the question is?). You feature this on the front page of your website (in fact, you should have the ability to capture information on *every* page of your site) and make it available to them in exchange for their name and email.

When they download your Free Report, you have just started them through The Alphabet Maze. Next, they'll receive a series of pre-written emails from you because you have installed an Auto-Responder system to further educate and motivate them to take action. As they begin to know, like and trust you through the messages that you send, you suddenly become their "WHO" and they do business with you.

Additionally, you modify your business card to promote this Free Report. That's much more interesting than your business address. Now you are attracting people in two different ways using the same Free Report. That's called Simultaneous action.

You then begin to feature this Free Report in all of your advertising – newspaper, fliers, radio, outdoor, magazines, invoices, brochures, car wraps and magnets, both the ones on your company vehicles and the ones that people put on their refrigerators. Anywhere you can promote this, you promote it.

Pretty soon, people get used to the fact that you are always providing good information for FREE (Don't you just love that word?!). You can change your Free Report every month, or have a variety of them available at the same time. The Strategy is to have some CHEESE that you can offer to ATTRACT the right type of "critter" so that you can win their heart, build a relationship and serve their needs.

This is just one Customer Attraction System that you can put in place. There are many others. They take every shape and size imaginable, but they all have the same objective in mind – Attracting Customers on autopilot. When you continually fill the funnel, your business will continually grow. One way to do this is by implementing a Customer Attraction System.

3. *Lost Customer Reactivation Campaign*

Losing customers is part of business. Earlier in this book we articulated the 6 reasons why people stop doing business with you. Of those, 4 of them you can do something about. Here is a proven strategy for regaining some of those lost customers.

Remember that Lost Customers represent the 3rd easiest type of customer to get to do business with you. The first are your current customers, then referrals. Lost customers come in 3rd because they already have some experience with you. And since the vast majority of them have stopped doing business with you for reasons that you can overcome, and since you now know the Lifetime Value of each of these customers, you should focus some of your time and energy in reactivating these most precious customers.

One way to do this is to have a series of three letters that you send to them. These aren't your normal, run of the mill letters mind you. These need to be a bit different. They need to grab their attention, change their perspective and get them to consider you once again.

One of the most effective ways to accomplish this is through the use of a 3D mail campaign.

What is 3D mail you ask????

It's just what it sounds like. It's *dimensional* mail. It's mail that has bulk, interesting items, and a curiosity factor. It's mail that gets their ATTENTION.

An associate of mine, Travis Lee, runs a company that provides many items just like this. And they have specific items developed for a Lost Customer Retention Campaign. You can learn about this at: www.3DMailResults.com.

Here's one example (and the components) of a multi-step direct mail Customer Re-Activation Campaign that is available from Travis' company. There's no doubt that this will capture the attention of your past customers, and you'll be pleasantly surprised at how much business this brings you, and how many other people they will tell about this mailing.

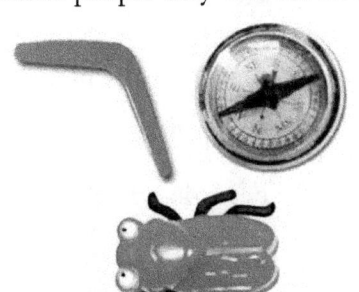

If you are serious about re-gaining lost customers, then you really should give this a try.

Each of these 3D items will fit in an envelope with a 1-2 page letter.

Step 1: Send a 10" Boomerang to them

Headline: **We Want You Back!**

Then, 7–10 days later

Step 2: Send them a Compass

Headline: **We've Been Looking for You!**

Then, 7–10 days later

Step 3: Send them a Plastic Bug

Headline: **"This is the Last Time I'm Going to Bug You"**

Do you think this will get some attention???

You bet it will. And because it's so different from anything your (former) customer has ever seen, they'll remember it…and YOU. Most of the time their reaction will be very positive. You're doing something to bring a smile to their face. It's a way to add personality to your marketing (a tactic that's super effective).

Most letters you receive are standard blah, blah, blah. Don't fall into that trap. BE DIFFERENT! BE DARING! BE UNIQUE!

You have nothing to lose – especially with a customer who is already not doing business with you.

Part of your job is to develop systems that you can implement at a moment's notice. This Lost Customer Re-Activation Campaign works phenomenally well.

You can make this part of your Automated Sales Force by setting it up one time, and then simply executing it as needed. No need to reinvent the wheel. Find what works, model it, and implement it. Track your results, tweak as needed and resend.

4. *Current Customer Retention Campaign*

The easiest way to keep your current customers coming back is to proactively retain them by staying in front of them. This is most easily accomplished through a regular printed newsletter. I say "regular" because it doesn't have to be monthly, though I'm a big fan of that.

A printed newsletter doesn't even have to be all about you. In fact, the best ones are NOT all about you. They have engaging activities, human-interest stories that have nothing to do with your business, and fun tidbits. Sure, there's space to talk about you—but you should focus most of it on THEM (think CHEESE).

Of course, if you want them to simply move your newsletter from the mailbox to the garbage can, then talk about you. If you want to engage them with it, then make it interesting and *talk about THEM*. And by all means, have some type of offer that they can benefit from (and you can profit from).

You can grow your RETAIN Stage significantly by sending a regular printed newsletter to your existing customers, but this can be a daunting task. That's why I've partnered with a company that will do most of the work for you. Find out more about this done-for-you system at www.MichaelDeLon.com.

There you go... four Automated Sales Force components you can use to Grow Your Business. Find out more about this done-for-you system by sending me an email at Michael@PaperbackExpert.com.

Chapter 26

A Sales Person Who is Never A Bother

If you were to hire a sales force to go out and meet with prospects, how much of their sales presentation would you want them to give?

You'd be livid if you found out that they were leaving out ANY of the presentation! How absurd. Any salesperson worth their weight is going to tell the entire story.

If that's the case, then why do you insist on not telling your entire story or giving your full presentation when you advertise? Why are your ads not filled with benefit after benefit and offer after offer? Why do you run 30-second radio ads instead of 60-second ads? Why do you not tell your entire story online and offline? Why do you wait until you are face to face with a prospect to let them know all they need to know?

Why, Why, Why????

The standard answer is: People won't read a long sales letter. Or, People won't watch a video longer than two minutes. Hogwash!

Length is irrelevant when the content is compelling!

If you have something to say that will interest your prospect, they'll invest hours. Say for example that you wanted to buy a new car. You pick the make and model. How much would you be willing to read, watch and listen to so that you can know everything about that car? You'd spend hours, days, sometimes months researching, reading magazines, watching videos, visiting the dealership, taking test drives and having long conversations with people who are experts about that specific car. If you were to find a new source of information that you could trust, you'd devour all you could to make sure you had all the information.

You can do the exact same thing with a sales letter. This can become your best salesperson. It never gets tired, takes no breaks, doesn't complain and can consistently deliver results month after month. And because you control the message, you determine exactly what is communicated each and every time. Nothing gets left out. Every objection is handled, every benefit presented and every order asked for. It really is a beautiful thing when done right.

Learning to write great copy is a skill that you can learn and master. It does take work, but there are ways to automate this process so that you aren't doing everything. It all depends on where you want to invest your time and energy.

If you've never considered using a "silent sales force", you should consider it. It will eliminate cold calling, guarantee full delivery of your message, and is extremely trackable.

There are dozens of books that can get you started, but the best one in my opinion is *The Ultimate Sales Letter* by Dan Kennedy. He takes you step by step through the process of not only writing your sales letter, but also choosing your best market.

Or you can hire a professional copywriter. The investment will more than pay for itself in the results you receive.

A sales letter can be as simple or complex as you want to make it, but it will definitely help you grow your business without being a bother.

Chapter 27

The Right Way To Write

Since you now see the value of using a sales letter, here is a sales letter writing mini course. Listed below are the basics of a good sales letter. There are a lot more techniques and strategies you can learn, but these dozen will get you headed in the "write" direction.

1. Select Your Market Carefully – Remember the Marketing Triad? Choosing your Market is THE most important success factor in a successful campaign. You'll have very little success selling hair care products to bald men.

2. Create a Compelling Message.

3. Have a Great Offer. The offer must have a deadline or it isn't an offer.

4. Craft a Headline that communicates the major benefit.

5. Make it NOT look like a sales letter – be personal. Make it look and feel like a human wrote it. Write like you speak.

6. Use normal, conversational language. Sometimes the best thing to do is to record your sales presentation and then transcribe it.

7. Have a very clear call to action. Tell them *exactly* what you want them to do and how you want them to respond.

8. Use a 24/7 Free Recorded Message as a next step.

9. Be sure to have a 100% Risk Free Guarantee.

10. Use a P.S. to restate your offer and deadline.

11. Send a 3D item with your letter to get it noticed.

12. Do a multi-step campaign to increase results—at least 3 mailings to the same market within 21 days.

Follow these steps when writing a sales letter (or any marketing piece for that matter) and your results will increase, your business will grow, and your profits will be "write" where you want them.

Chapter 28

Brochures, Business Cards & Other Throwaways

I'm not a huge fan of dog tags. I know they serve their purpose, but beyond that they can be pretty useless.

The "dog tags" I'm referring to are not the kind used to identify military personnel. I'm referring to those identifiers that we all "wear" to communicate what we do.

Almost everyone has a business card. Heavens, even my 14-year-old son has a business card for his lawn mowing business. And come to think about it, he has a brochure as well. Now his are a bit different than most, but still, he has them.

Most business cards contain name, rank and serial number. They are basic, banal, and blah. Their primary use is as a memory aid while talking to someone new so that you remember their name until your conversation is over.

And brochures are some of the biggest waste of paper on earth. Do you really think that people are that interested in your company and products? Remember: They are only interested in What's In It For Me?, and more often than not, your brochure isn't answering that question.

So what are you to do, throw these all away? No, don't do that. Instead, you should repurpose them so that they communicate in a way that's engaging and memorable. You can use your business card as a lead-in to your 24/7 Free Recorded Message or to download your Free Report (or to receive a free copy of your book) at your website. Your business card should be primarily about your prospect and secondarily about you.

Why are you in business anyway? Isn't it to serve others? What better way to serve your future customers than by giving them a business card that will move them a step closer to actually doing business with you!

It may take a bit of thought on your part – and it will definitely take some courage – but when you hand someone your business card and it gives them an immediate benefit, not only will it begin to position you as different, it will cause them to know, like and trust you more. That is a great thing!

So look at your business card and brochures. Try to see them from your prospect's eyes. What's In It For Them? Consider these questions:

> What is it that you are communicating?
> WHY should they care?
> What are you doing for them?
> How can you help them?

These are the questions you need to be asking yourself (and your staff) on a regular basis. *Stay focused on your customer.* **Offer them CHEESE** at every opportunity.

Use your business cards and brochures not as throwaway items, but as a Customer Attraction System that will help you to grow your business.

Consider what it is that your customer is actually paying for. Find ways to promote that on your business cards, brochures and other throwaway items and watch your business begin to grow.

Chapter 29

The 5 Critical Questions

Before you embark on any journey, especially a business or marketing journey, you need to clearly answer these 5 questions. They will clarify for you precisely what you are doing and why you are doing it. Believe me, you'll come back to these time after time.

➢ What do you want to make happen?

➢ What are you up against?

➢ What do you have to work with?

➢ What makes sense?

➢ How will you Measure Success?

All of these are simple questions that can have complex answers. When you need clarity, get away for a few minutes, ask yourself these questions, write down your answers, and get back to work.

If you've never done anything like this before you're in good company. No one else around you has either. Don't let that stop you. Do what you know is right and the results will follow.

Chapter 30

Your Annual Marketing Calendar

One of the most basic of all systems is usually completely ignored by the average business owner. It seems that no one wants to commit their plans to writing, but *this one simple action will accelerate your growth by leaps and bounds.*

Marketing is not an event; it's a process. We've discussed a myriad of processes throughout this book; all are focused on helping you grow your business. But without this particular process in place, you will wander aimlessly and only achieve a portion of your capacity.

Creating a marketing calendar is quite simple. I typically use a spreadsheet.

Just list the months along the top and every promotion that you will do along the left side. You should also list the type of media that you will use with each promotion.

Crafting an Annual Marketing Calendar will enable you to see and seize opportunities that you would not normally observe. You'll anticipate holidays and be able to plan more holistically. The benefits you'll receive are innumerable.

Setting aside a day or two to plan your entire next year is one of THE highest pay-off activities you will ever do. Putting it off won't help your business to grow. You need to plan for your growth.

You should do it NOW!

Chapter 31

The 30-Day Challenge

I have a challenge for you. For the next 30 days, I want you to read no other business book, newsletter or ezine. **I want you to FOCUS** all of your energies to master what you've learned in these pages on marketing.

So write today's date in the margin on this page. Commit to pore over these pages and mine them for all the gold that's hidden beneath the surface (there's a lot here!). Take time each day to read, think and plan what it is that you can do to **apply one thing from each chapter every day**.

It might be setting up your 24/7 Free Recorded Message. Or perhaps you need to carve out your positioning. How about creating a 100% Risk Free Guarantee? You could even do something as simple as putting in place a post-sale "thank you" campaign that includes a personal, hand-written "thank you" followed by an email or two. You can never go wrong showing your appreciation.

> *You* have to decide what you are going to do.
>
> But do *something*!

Take *The 30-Day Challenge* seriously. Set 2-3 definite objectives. Involve your staff. Tell your family, friends, and most importantly, tell your customers!

People want you to succeed. Are you ready to do your part?

As you embark on this journey, you're going to have to decide to stop playing games with your future and become a serious student of marketing. Remember that your #1 job is to become a Master of Marketing; that will require some time and study. This is why the 30-Day Challenge is so important to your growth—both personally and for your company.

Most business owners play around with marketing like a tourist plays around in the casino, throwing money away hoping for Lady Luck to show up and give them a much larger return for very little effort. That rarely happens.

The choice is yours. You can:

Take Your Chances Playing Advertising Roulette

 **Or**

Strategically Aim for the Marketing Bull's Eye

When you focus on what you want to accomplish, there's not much that can stop you from achieving it. Take The 30-Day Challenge and you'll create the momentum necessary to keep you going – and *growing* – month after month.

Conclusion

You now have a solid foundation upon which to construct your own marketing program. You've been given the strategies, concepts and tactics to build your business. And you have the blueprint formula to view your business in its Three Stages.

Now it's time for you to go to work.

If you haven't done so already, go back through the **Marketing Audit**. Answer it honestly and find out exactly where you are right now. Then break down your business into **The Three Stages of Business**; consider how you want to bring your customers through **The Alphabet Maze** and work on the components in your **Marketing Triad**.

This is where most people fall off. They read a book like this and say, "I'll get to that tomorrow" and put the book on their desk. A few weeks later they find it under a stack of papers, briefly flip through it, then put it on the shelf with a dozen or more other "good intention" books that they've read.

> Your business won't change until *you* do something to change it.

You have to take action. You have to take what you've learned here – even if it's just one idea, concept or strategy – and **apply it** to your business.

I learned these phrases early in my sales career and they have served me well ever since:

❝Education Without Action is Entertainment.❞

"To Know and Not to Do is Not to Know."

My time management philosophy is: **Do It Now!**

If you lack motivation, take a few moments to visualize the future you desire. What will it be like when you are Attracting customers on autopilot, Engaging with them profitably, and Retaining them for Life? How will your life change when your sales, profits and income are continually rising, even in "bad economic times"? What is it that you really want your life to be like?

It's possible! But it requires discipline, focus and *action*.

As you begin to create your marketing, don't worry about getting it perfect. It doesn't need to be. *Get it done and get it out.*

Begin The 30-Day Challenge and set some realistic yet challenging goals. Don't bite off more than you can handle, but make it aggressive. You'll be surprised at how much you can accomplish when you have a dream, make a plan, and decide to let nothing stand in your way.

I hope that our paths cross someday so I can hear what you accomplished by implementing the strategies you learned from reading the book *On Marketing*.

Position Yourself to Profit,
Michael

A Special Offer

Complimentary *Paperback Expert* Assessment

This is a service we provide to help you discern if publishing a book can help you grow your business. This complimentary 30-minute Author Interview will help you more fully understand our process, review your book ideas and consider possible marketing strategies and timelines.

If, after that call, you desire to move forward, then we'll lay out the project, agree upon the direction and finalize the details. As you leave that meeting, the calendar begins to turn and before you realize, you will be a *Paperback Expert*.

Request Your Complimentary *Paperback Expert* Assessment at www.PaperbackExpert.com/PEA.

Recommended Resources

On Marketing is filled with numerous resources that you can use to grow your business. Here's a list of my favorites:

Books

The E-Myth, Michael Gerber
FREE, Chris Anderson
Customers for Life, Carl Sewell
The Ultimate Sales Letter, Dan Kennedy
The Wizard of Ads Trilogy, Roy H. Williams

Copywriting & Direct Mail

3D Mail – Travis Lee (*www.3dMailResults.com*)
Dan Kennedy – *www.dankennedy.com*
Roy Williams – *www.MondayMorningMemo.com*

Thanks for reading…

About the Author

Michael DeLon is the founder of Paperback Expert.

He's an author, marketing strategist and business growth coach who specializes in helping small businesspeople build trust as they position themselves as *The Expert* by publishing their own book. Then Michael teaches them how to use their book to Attract, Engage and Retain customers for life while stimulating Referrals.

He's a straight shooter with over 25 years of experience studying, applying, and fine-tuning these marketing strategies. His vast experience allows him to find unique solutions to his clients' challenges that others never see.

Marketing doesn't have to be a gamble. Michael can help you step away from the Advertising Roulette Wheel and Aim for the Marketing Bull's Eye. He can also help you build trust through authorship and become a recognized expert by helping you publish your own book!

Michael is the husband of one and father of three. He's a committed follower of Jesus Christ and is deeply involved in his church. You can normally find Michael investing time with his family or helping others grow in their marketing and their marriage relationship.

Contact Michael via: *Michael@PaperbackExpert.com.*